OPPOSING VIEWPOINTS® SERIES

Alcohol

Other Books of Related Interest:

Opposing Viewpoints Series

Addiction

At Issue Series

Alcohol Abuse

Drunk Driving

"Congress shall make no law . . . abridging the freedom of speech, or of the press."

First Amendment to the U.S. Constitution

The basic foundation of our democracy is the First Amendment guarantee of freedom of expression. The Opposing Viewpoints series is dedicated to the concept of this basic freedom and the idea that it is more important to practice it than to enshrine it.

OPPOSING VIEWPOINTS® SERIES

Alcohol

Andrea C. Nakaya, Book Editor

GREENHAVEN PRESS

An imprint of Thomson Gale, a part of The Thomson Corporation

Detroit • New York • San Francisco • New Haven, Conn. • Waterville, Maine • London

Christine Nasso, *Publisher*
Elizabeth Des Chenes, *Managing Editor*

© 2008 The Gale Group.

Star logo is a trademark and Gale and Greenhaven Press are registered trademarks used herein under license.

For more information, contact:
Greenhaven Press
27500 Drake Rd.
Farmington Hills, MI 48331-3535
Or you can visit our Internet site at http://www.gale.com

Cover photograph reproduced by permission of photos.com.

LIBRARY OF CONGRESS CATALOGING-IN-PUBLICATION DATA

Alcohol / Andrea C. Nakaya, book editor.
    p. cm. -- (Opposing Viewpoints)
    Includes bibliographical references and index.
    ISBN-13: 978-0-7377-3733-2 (hardcover)
    ISBN-13: 978-0-7377-3734-9 (pbk.)
    1. Alcoholism--Juvenile literature. 2. Alcohol--Physiological effect--Juvenile literature. 3. Drinking of alcoholic beverages--Juvenile literature. I. Nakaya, Andrea C., 1976-
    HV5066.A39 2008
    362.292--dc22

                           2007029294

ISBN-10: 0-7377-3733-6 (hardcover)
ISBN-10: 0-7377-3734-4 (pbk.)

Printed in the United States of America
10 9 8 7 6 5 4 3 2 1

Contents

Chapter 3: What Are the Causes of Alcohol Abuse?

Chapter 4: What Measures Should Be Taken to Reduce Alcohol-Related Problems?

Why Consider Opposing Viewpoints?

> "The only way in which a human being can make some approach to knowing the whole of a subject is by hearing what can be said about it by persons of every variety of opinion and studying all modes in which it can be looked at by every character of mind. No wise man ever acquired his wisdom in any mode but this."
>
> John Stuart Mill

In our media-intensive culture it is not difficult to find differing opinions. Thousands of newspapers and magazines and dozens of radio and television talk shows resound with differing points of view. The difficulty lies in deciding which opinion to agree with and which "experts" seem the most credible. The more inundated we become with differing opinions and claims, the more essential it is to hone critical reading and thinking skills to evaluate these ideas. Opposing Viewpoints books address this problem directly by presenting stimulating debates that can be used to enhance and teach these skills. The varied opinions contained in each book examine many different aspects of a single issue. While examining these conveniently edited opposing views, readers can develop critical thinking skills such as the ability to compare and contrast authors' credibility, facts, argumentation styles, use of persuasive techniques, and other stylistic tools. In short, the Opposing Viewpoints series is an ideal way to attain the higher-level thinking and reading skills so essential in a culture of diverse and contradictory opinions.

In addition to providing a tool for critical thinking, Opposing Viewpoints books challenge readers to question their own strongly held opinions and assumptions. Most people form their opinions on the basis of upbringing, peer pressure, and personal, cultural, or professional bias. By reading carefully balanced opposing views, readers must directly confront new ideas as well as the opinions of those with whom they disagree. This is not to simplistically argue that everyone who reads opposing views will—or should—change his or her opinion. Instead, the series enhances readers' understanding of their own views by encouraging confrontation with opposing ideas. Careful examination of others' views can lead to the readers' understanding of the logical inconsistencies in their own opinions, perspective on why they hold an opinion, and the consideration of the possibility that their opinion requires further evaluation.

Evaluating Other Opinions

To ensure that this type of examination occurs, Opposing Viewpoints books present all types of opinions. Prominent spokespeople on different sides of each issue as well as well-known professionals from many disciplines challenge the reader. An additional goal of the series is to provide a forum for other, less-known, or even unpopular viewpoints. The opinion of an ordinary person who has had to make the decision to cut off life support from a terminally ill relative, for example, may be just as valuable and provide just as much insight as a medical ethicist's professional opinion. The editors have two additional purposes in including these less-known views. One, the editors encourage readers to respect others' opinions—even when not enhanced by professional credibility. It is only by reading or listening to and objectively evaluating others' ideas that one can determine whether they are worthy of consideration. Two, the inclusion of such viewpoints encourages the important critical thinking skill of objectively evaluating an author's credentials and bias. This evaluation will illuminate an author's reasons for taking a particular stance on an issue and will aid in readers' evaluation of the author's ideas.

It is our hope that these books will give readers a deeper understanding of the issues debated and an appreciation of the complexity of even seemingly simple issues when good and honest people disagree. This awareness is particularly important in a democratic society such as ours in which people enter into public debate to determine the common good. Those with whom one disagrees should not be regarded as enemies but rather as people whose views deserve careful examination and may shed light on one's own.

Thomas Jefferson once said that "difference of opinion leads to inquiry, and inquiry to truth." Jefferson, a broadly educated man, argued that "if a nation expects to be ignorant and free . . . it expects what never was and never will be." As individuals and as a nation, it is imperative that we consider the opinions of others and examine them with skill and discernment. The Opposing Viewpoints series is intended to help readers achieve this goal.

David L. Bender and Bruno Leone,
Founders

Introduction

> "*You may not speak the language, you may not understand the culture—but wherever you are in the world tonight, you will be able to get a drink.*"
>
> *—Nick Brownlee,*
> *author*

According to a July 2006 Gallup poll, 64 percent of Americans ages eighteen and older say they drink alcoholic beverages. Alcohol use is also very common in most other countries around the world. There is continuing debate over whether alcohol is harmful or beneficial to health and society, but as the Gallup poll illustrates, the fact is that regardless of such controversy, this drug is widely consumed.

The World Health Organization (WHO) reports that alcohol use is widespread around the globe and has increased in recent decades. It reports: "Alcohol use is deeply embedded in many societies, and about 2000 million people drink alcohol in most parts of the world." Alcohol use has been prevalent in the United States for many years. According to Gallup statistics, the percentage of Americans who use it has changed little over the past sixty years, averaging about 63 percent of people age eighteen and older.

Certain segments of the population are more likely than others to consume alcohol. Numerous national and international studies show that men are more likely to drink than women, and are also more likely to drink large amounts of alcohol. For example, the U.S. Department of Health and Human Services (HHS) says that in a study of nineteen to thirty year olds, 45 percent of men and compared to only 26.7 percent of women reported heavy drinking in the past two weeks.

The agency also reports on the relationship between ethnicity and alcohol consumption, finding that, "In general white and Native American young adults drink more than African Americans and Asians, and drinking rates for Hispanics fall in the middle." According to HHS, those in the military are also more likely to drink alcohol.

Youth alcohol consumption is also very common. In the United States, despite the fact that consumption by those under age twenty-one is illegal, alcohol is the most commonly used drug among youth. The Substance Abuse and Mental Health Services Administration (SAMHSA) estimates that in 2004 28.7 percent of youth consumed alcohol in the month prior to being surveyed. The National Institute on Alcohol Abuse and Alcoholism reports that by eighth grade, 41 percent of American children have tried alcohol, and by tenth grade this percentage rises to 62 percent. Rules on youth alcohol consumption vary in other countries, but WHO finds that in general, youth drinking is widespread. In 2003 the European School Survey Project on Alcohol and Other Drugs conducted its third survey, consisting of thirty-five European countries, and found that at least 90 percent of youth surveyed had drunk alcohol at least once in their lifetime. "However," it cautions, "These students do not all drink on a regular basis." Researchers found that regular drinkers ranged from a high of 43 to 50 percent in the United Kingdom, Denmark, Austria, and the Czech Republic, to a low of 7 percent in Turkey.

Youth drinkers are more likely than adults to consume a large amount of alcohol at one time, a pattern often referred to as binge drinking. WHO finds that, "There appears to be an international pattern towards . . . drinking to intoxication. . . . Internationally . . . an important current feature of young people's drinking is the importance of the 'buzz'. Many young people now drink in order to get drunk." In the United States, SAMHSA found that in 2004 more than 7 million underage youth had engaged in binge drinking in the past month. HHS agrees that a large number of youth engage in binge drinking. It says, "It's not only that young people are drinking but the way they drink that puts them at . . . high risk for alcohol-related problems. . . . Young adults are especially likely to binge drink and to drink heavily." Yet others maintain that such drinking patterns involve only a minority of youth. For example, in a 2006 issue of the *Scientist,* researcher Richard Rice states, "College students consistently overestimate the extent to which their peers engage in high risk drinking. . . . In point of fact, the norm among college students is to drink moderately if at all."

People drink alcohol for a great variety of reasons. It is an integral part of many important social occasions that mark births, deaths, and weddings. It is also frequently present at social events such as sporting events and parties. Says journalist Roger Scruton in the *New Statesman,* "Even though alcohol is a huge threat to health, safety and society. Drink is part of our culture." One reason drinking is so popular is that it reduces people's inhibitions and makes them feel relaxed and at ease. According to the Institute of Medicine, "Both adolescents and adults indicate that alcohol is an important ingredient in social interactions, allowing them to lower their inhibitions and feel more relaxed in social situations." However some people consume alcohol because they develop an addiction to it. SAMHSA estimates that 7.6 percent of Americans age twelve or older meet the criteria for alcohol dependence or abuse. For example, in a 2006 interview in *People Weekly,* Toren Volkmann warns that many youth become addicted to alcohol and cannot stop consuming it. "It's important for parents not to look at teen drinking as just a rite of passage," he insists.

Alcohol is widely available and consumed and has a profound impact on society. There is heated disagreement about whether it is harmful or beneficial. As the Mayo Clinic points out: "For every article you read about the benefits of alcohol consumption, another seems to warn you of its risks." In *Opposing Viewpoints: Alcohol*, the authors offer various perspectives on this contentious subject in the following chapters: How Does Alcohol Use Affect Health? Is Alcohol Use Harmful to Society? What Are the Causes of Alcohol Abuse? What Measures Should Be Taken to Reduce Alcohol-Related Problems? As the debate continues, people around the world continue to consume alcohol.

CHAPTER 1

How Does Alcohol Use Affect Health?

Chapter Preface

According to the American Association of Suicidology (AAS), the risk of suicide among alcoholics is 50 to 70 percent higher than in the general population. AAS is only one among many groups that maintain alcohol abuse is a cause of suicide. However, others contend that there is no evidence for such a conclusion. The dispute forms part of a larger debate over how alcohol use affects health in general.

There are numerous studies that link alcohol consumption—particularly heavy consumption—with suicide. According to the authors of a 2005 article in *Preventing Suicide*: "Decades of research strongly suggest that alcohol is a contributing factor in scores of suicides for both men and women." A recent example of such research is a 2006 study by the Centre for Addiction and Mental Health, which found that as alcohol consumption levels rise, suicide rates increase as well. The researchers observed this link for total alcohol consumption and for consumption of beer, wine, or spirits separately.

Experts believe there are various possible reasons for the link between alcohol consumption and suicide. The most common explanation is that because alcohol has a depressant effect on the brain and also reduces inhibitions and alters judgment, suicide is more likely to occur. *TeensHealth*, a Web site created by the Nemours Foundation, concurs: "Alcohol and some drugs have depressive effects on the brain. Misuse of these substances can bring on serious depression. . . . In addition to their depressive effects, alcohol and drugs alter a person's judgment. They interfere with the ability to assess risk, make good choices, and think of solutions to problems. Many suicide attempts occur when a person is under the influence of alcohol or drugs."

Critics contend that although researchers have observed an association between alcohol consumption and suicide, there is no evidence that drinking actually causes a person to end his or her life. For example, the online *Suicide Reference Library* reports that while there is a correlation between alcohol use and suicide, "The exact nature of alcohol's role in suicide is unclear." Such critics point out that although people who commit suicide often consume alcohol, the alcohol is not necessarily the cause of the suicide. They argue that people who abuse alcohol often have other problems such as financial and family difficulties that may contribute to suicide, or they may have a personality type that simply makes them more likely to commit suicide. Says the New York State Office of Mental Health, "Substance use and abuse can be common among persons prone to be impulsive, and among persons who engage in many types of high-risk behaviors that result in self-harm."

As a legal and widely used drug, alcohol is subject to extensive debate concerning its effects on human health. Suicide is only one of the health threats linked to alcohol consumption. In addition to its possible harms, there is evidence that alcohol consumption may also be beneficial to human health. While there is a wealth of information on alcohol's health effects, there is a lack of agreement on how to interpret this information. The authors in the following chapter offer various responses to this much debated issue.

> "Numerous studies have demonstrated
> ... [a relationship between] moderate
> consumption of alcoholic beverages ...
> [and] a significant reduction in the risk
> of heart disease."

Moderate Alcohol Consumption Reduces the Risk of Heart Disease

Weinberg Group

In the following viewpoint the Weinberg Group concludes that moderate alcohol consumption reduces the risk of coronary heart disease. Numerous studies show this to be the case regardless of beverage type, insists the author. According to the Weinberg Group, the greatest benefits occur with the consumption of small amounts of alcohol several times per week, and among those individuals who are already at risk for cardiovascular disease. The Weinberg Group is an international scientific and regulatory consulting firm. It prepared this report at the request of the Brewers of Europe, an organization that represents the European brewing industry.

Weinberg Group, "Background Review—Risks and Benefits of Alcohol Consumption. The Role of Moderate Drinking," *An Independent Review of Issues Related to Alcohol Consumption in Europe: Prepared for the Brewers of Europe*, June 12, 2006, p. 41–47. www.weinberggroup.com. Reproduced by permission.

As you read, consider the following questions:

1. At what level of consumption is the greatest benefit on coronary heart disease achieved, according to the Weinberg Group?

2. As stated by the author, what are some of the industrialized nations where the cardioprotective effect of moderate alcohol consumption has been observed?

3. What has research shown about exclusive moderate drinkers of beer in Germany, according to the Weinberg Group?

The risks associated with excessive alcohol consumption are well known. Compared to non-drinkers, heavy drinkers are at increased risk of chronic diseases such as liver cancer, cirrhosis, and upper digestive cancers. In addition, heavy drinkers are more likely to die from injuries, violence, and suicide than non-drinkers. Alcohol abuse also has negative effects on non-drinkers; for example, pregnant women who consume heavy amounts of alcohol may have babies with long-term problems such as foetal alcohol syndrome. Finally, heavy alcohol consumption is implicated in a significant portion of motor vehicle accidents in certain countries.

Despite the significant negative consequences associated with excessive alcohol consumption, researchers have long recognised that alcohol's effects are dose-related, and that the effects of low and moderate doses of alcohol are quite different from those noted above. Beneficial health and social effects of moderate consumption have been suggested for centuries. However, most of the rigorous scientific research has been conducted in the past few decades.

The relationship between moderate alcohol consumption and reduced risk of coronary heart disease (CHD) was first documented scientifically in the 1970s. This was followed by interest in what was termed the 'French Paradox,' the observation that Mediterranean populations that consumed high overall levels of red wine had low CHD despite their high intake of saturated fat. Since that time, research into the beneficial effects of moderate alcohol consumption has been extensive. Numerous studies have demonstrated a wide range of benefits associated with moderate consumption of alcoholic beverages; the most widely accepted of these benefits is a significant reduction in the risk of heart disease.

What is Moderate Consumption?

There is no universally accepted definition of 'moderate consumption.' Examination of the literature indicates that the definition of moderate drinking varies by study, by author, by country, by gender, by age, and by beverage type. For example, the standard drink size in Europe ranges from 8 to 12 grams of alcohol, whereas it is about 14 grams in the United States. Despite these differences, there is a general consensus that moderate consumption can be recognised and that it can be distinguished from heavy drinking. A number of authors have defined moderate drinking as an average consumption of about 1 to 2 drinks per day or up to about 30 grams alcohol per day. . . .

When considering moderate drinking, the pattern of consumption is also important. There is evidence that the greatest benefits of moderate drinking occur when there is regular moderate consumption rather than sporadic episodes of heavy drinking. There is also a suggestion that drinking alcohol with a meal rather than on an empty stomach is beneficial. It must also be noted that there are some populations for whom even moderate drinking is inappropriate: individuals who are at risk of addiction or abuse; pregnant women; and people who are driving motor vehicles, operating machinery or taking certain medicines. . . .

Moderate Consumption and Coronary Heart Disease

Coronary heart disease is the leading cause of death in many westernised countries. The relationship between moderate alcohol consumption and coronary heart disease (CHD) was first documented scientifically in the 1970s by investigators at [managed care organization] Kaiser Permanente in California. Since that time, an abundance of observational epidemiology studies ... and short-term human experimental studies have confirmed the cardioprotective effects of moderate alcohol consumption. Evidence from more than one hundred epidemiologic studies involving hundreds of thousands of subjects has led many researchers to conclude that the association is causal in nature.

Relationship Is a J-Shaped Curve

The relationship between alcohol consumption and CHD mortality is often described as a 'J-shaped' or 'U-shaped' curve. This describes a relationship in which the highest mortality is seen among heavy drinkers; the next highest among abstainers; and the lowest among moderate drinkers. The depth and width of the risk curve varies somewhat, depending on the underlying CHD risk of the population being studied. That is, those at highest risk of CHD derive the greatest benefit from moderate alcohol intake. . . .

The level of consumption that has been associated with decreased risk of CHD varies from study to study (from about 1 drink per day to about 3 drinks per day), but it appears that the greatest benefit is achieved at about one-half to one drink per day, and that the risk does not decline appreciably with increased intake. A recent meta-analysis of fifty-one high-quality studies published between 1966 and 1998 showed that the maximum protective effect occurred at 10 grams ethanol per day (less than 1 drink) in women and 25 grams per day (about 2 drinks) in men. The benefit is a substantial one: the reduction in risk of CHD associated with light to moderate drinking is estimated to be about 30 to 50%.

This J-shaped curve also emphasises the fact that high levels of alcohol consumption are associated with increased risk of heart disease. Consistent heavy alcohol consumption is known to be related to cardiomyopathy, congestive heart failure, and arrhythmias.

As noted previously, pattern of consumption is important. It appears that the protective effect is related more strongly to frequency of consumption than to volume; consumption of small amounts several times per week reduces risk more than the same volume consumed on few occasions.

Benefits Are Robust

The cardioprotective effect of moderate alcohol consumption is remarkably consistent. The benefit has been demonstrated in both men and women, although it is greatest among those whose age puts them at highest cardiovascular risk (i.e., men over age 45 and women over age 55). It is seen in most industrialised nations, including those in Europe, North America, and Australia, China and Japan. The beneficial effect is observed independent of smoking status and body mass index. The benefit has been confirmed in studies of varying designs that have adjusted for various confounding factors. It has been observed whether the study endpoint is both fatal and nonfatal CHD. Finally, moderate alcohol consumption appears to confer CHD benefits among high-risk populations (i.e., individuals who have diabetes, hypertension, or previous myocardial infarction).

Benefits Occur Regardless of Beverage Type

Early studies suggested that red wine might be more beneficial to the heart than other types of alcoholic beverages. While there may still be some public perception that this is true, more recent [as of 2006] scientific studies have clearly demonstrated that all types of alcoholic beverages confer cardiovascular benefits. In cultures where a particular alcohol beverage is consumed by a majority of drinkers, studies usually show

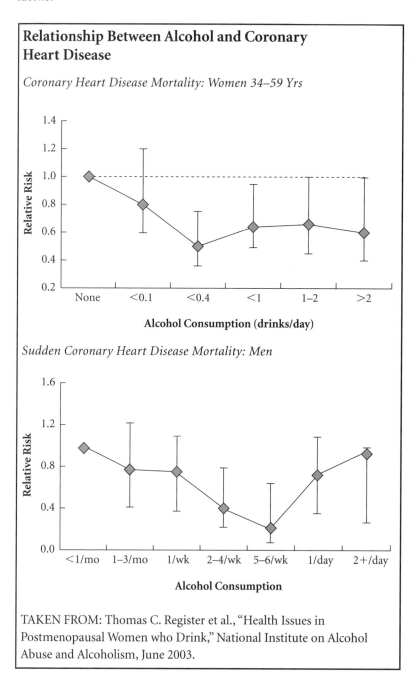

Relationship Between Alcohol and Coronary Heart Disease

Coronary Heart Disease Mortality: Women 34–59 Yrs

Sudden Coronary Heart Disease Mortality: Men

TAKEN FROM: Thomas C. Register et al., "Health Issues in Postmenopausal Women who Drink," National Institute on Alcohol Abuse and Alcoholism, June 2003.

that beverage as being associated with the greatest CHD benefit. For example, in Germany where beer is the most commonly consumed beverage, research has shown protection against CHD to be especially strong among exclusive moderate drinkers of beer.

Specific alcoholic beverages also contain numerous substances other than ethanol that may exert additional cardioprotective effects. For example, red and white wines contain many bioactive polyphenolic compounds, including flavonoids and antioxidants. Beer contains amino acids, peptides, B vitamins, as well as phenolic compounds derived from hops and malts. Research shows that homocysteine[1] levels are lower among beer drinkers than among those who drink wine or spirits. This has been attributed to the high B vitamin content of beer. There is some indication that the antioxidants present in beer (including ferulic acid) may be more easily absorbed than those found in red wine.

However, it appears that the CHD benefits derive substantially from the alcohol content of the beverage, rather than any other components. A meta-analysis of cohort studies that involved more than 300,000 people followed for more than 1.8 million person-years concluded that if a particular type of alcoholic beverage afforded additional cardiovascular benefit apart from its alcoholic content, the benefit was likely to be modest at best or possibly restricted to certain subpopulations.

Relationship Is Not Explained by Confounding

Some have questioned whether there are other factors associated with alcohol consumption, rather than alcohol itself, that might account for the reduced risk of CHD. A number of possible explanations have been suggested (the non-drinkers group is contaminated by 'sick quitters,'[2] If many people in

1. High homocysteine levels are reported to be a risk factor for heart attack.
2. People who have stopped drinking because they have become sick.

poor health stop drinking this could lead to the remaining drinkers being healthier than the non-drinkers without alcohol causing the improved health. confounding influences of dietary, lifestyle, and socioeconomic factors; factors unique to specific beverage types, etc.). Extensive efforts have been made to investigate each of these possible confounders or alternative explanations, and a number of authors have stated definitively that the primary factor in the lower rates of CHD is alcohol itself.

Mechanisms for Alcohol's Beneficial Effects

There are a number of mechanisms by which moderate alcohol consumption exerts its beneficial effects on CHD. The most important ones are described below.

- Moderate alcohol improves the lipid profile. Alcohol increases high-density lipoprotein (HDL) cholesterol (the 'good' cholesterol) and inhibits oxidation of low-density lipoprotein (LDL) cholesterol (the 'bad' cholesterol).

- Moderate alcohol reduces risk of thromboses (or clots) [clots in blood vessels can cause strokes and heart attacks]. Alcohol reduces platelet aggregation, reduces fibrinogen levels, and increases fibrinolysis (the dissolving of clots).

- Moderate alcohol increases coronary blood flow and reduces blood pressure.

- Alcohol has beneficial effects on hormones. It reduces blood insulin, increases insulin sensitivity, and increases oestrogen levels.

- Moderate alcohol reduces stress.

- Alcohol also decreases plasma homocysteine, which is an independent risk factor for vascular diseases. . . .

Part of a Healthy Lifestyle for Many People

Excessive alcohol consumption is associated with significant negative health and social consequences, including increased risk of liver cancer, cirrhosis, and upper digestive cancers, injuries, violence, suicide, and motor vehicle accidents. However, numerous studies have demonstrated a range of benefits associated with moderate consumption of alcoholic beverages (1–2 drinks per day), including reduced risk of all-cause mortality; heart failure and myocardial infarction [heart attack]; ischemic stroke; diabetes and metabolic syndrome; and a number of benefits related to psychological well-being. The most widely accepted benefit is a significant reduction in the risk of coronary heart disease.

Coronary heart disease is the leading cause of death in many westernised countries. It has been estimated that moderate alcohol consumption could save 80,000 lives per year in the United States alone. The reduction in risk of CHD associated with light to moderate drinking is estimated to be about 30 to 50%. In contrast, high levels of alcohol consumption are associated with increased risk of heart disease.

Numerous studies suggest that CHD benefits derive from the alcohol content of the beverage, rather than any other components; however alcoholic beverages contain numerous other substances (e.g., antioxidants, vitamins, phenolic compounds) that may exert additional cardioprotective effects.

Moderate alcohol consumption is associated with a range of health and social benefits; however potential risks are associated with any level of alcohol consumption. Decisions about consumption of alcohol are complex and require a case-by-case evaluation of an individual's particular situation, perhaps in consultation with a physician. Individuals who are at risk of addiction or abuse, or who have certain medical, psychiatric, or pharmacologic contraindications, should abstain from alcoholic beverages. However, light to moderate alcohol consumption can be part of a healthy lifestyle for those who choose to consume.

| "I actually don't think . . . [light to moderate drinking] is good for your heart."

Moderate Alcohol Consumption May Not Reduce the Risk of Heart Disease

Rod Jackson, interviewed by Norman Swan

It is unlikely that there is a link between moderate drinking and a reduced risk of heart disease, argues Rod Jackson in the following viewpoint. In his opinion, studies showing such a link are not accounting for many of the other factors influencing heart disease. For example, says Jackson, moderate drinkers frequently do many other things in moderation, which is often good for their cardiovascular health. He concludes that only moderate to heavy drinking will actually benefit the heart, and that at such a level of consumption, the harm done to the rest of the body outweigh the benefits. Jackson is a professor of epidemiology at the University of Auckland, New Zealand.

As you read, consider the following questions:

1. According to the author, upon what type of data have all past studies of alcohol and heart disease been based?

2. What is moderate to heavy drinking, as defined by Jackson?

3. How does the author explain the "French paradox," which refers to the fact that the French have lower rates of heart disease despite their diet?

It's been widely assumed that a small amount of alcohol each day is good for your heart and helps to explain why, say, the French have less heart disease than us [Australians and New Zealanders] despite their diet.

Well a leading public health researcher has recanted and reckons a re-think is in order. It's probably only relatively heavy drinking that has the benefit for the heart he says, and then the costs are too great to make it worth trying.

Rod Jackson is Professor of Epidemiology at the University of Auckland and he published his views in *The Lancet*.

Rod Jackson: I've been working off and on now for about 20 years now and I got onto it by accident.

Norman Swan: This is what working in alcohol rather than on it?

Ah ha, working in research on alcohol for about 20 years. I first came across it when I was doing my PhD which was meant to be a study of the relationship between physical activity and coronary heart disease. And someone suggested that I include alcohol as a variable and when I was doing my analysis I found that it was the most powerful factor of my whole analysis. People who drank moderately had about half the risk of a heart attack as people who didn't and we did our best to see were there any biases in our analyses and we got pretty convinced that light to moderate drinking was good for you.

Not Recommended for Health

A number of strategies reduce the risk of chronic disease, including a healthful diet, physical activity, avoidance of smoking, and maintenance of a healthy weight. . . . It is not recommended that anyone begin drinking or drink more frequently on the basis of health considerations.

Department of Health and Human Services and the Department of Agriculture, "Dietary Guidelines for Americans 2005," January 12, 2005. www.healthierus.gov.

HRT Study

So what made you recant?

What got me to recant was the controversy over the hormone replacement therapy [HRT]. Through the first major study on hormone replacement therapy and heart disease, it was the 1990 publication of the Nurse's Health Study.

This is really a follow-up study of 120 odd thousand nurses from the 80s onwards.

That's it, actually from the mid 70s, they sent them a questionnaire every two years and have been following them up ever since looking at a whole lot of stuff. And one of their publications on the front page of the *New England Journal of Medicine* in the middle of 1990 and then I assume on the front page of the *New York Times* was that women who take hormone replacement therapy have half the risk of coronary disease as women who don't. Then in 1998 a randomised trial the [Heart and Estrogen/Progestin Replacement Study] HERS Study was published demonstrating that there was no effect of hormone replacement therapy on coronary disease. The difference being that the nurses' study was a standard observational cohort study where they asked the woman, do you take hormonal replacement therapy or not? So the women were kind

33

of self selected, they took it or not, whereas the HERS Study was a trial where women were actually randomised, they couldn't choose whether they got hormone replacement therapy or a placebo. And when they did it that way they found no effect. And it really made me rethink.

Moderation Extends Beyond Drinking

Because nobody's done a randomised trial of alcohol, it's all been observational?

Exactly. But what is really interesting is that the same nurses' heath study that showed the HRT effect has published a similar paper looking at alcohol and found a 50% reduction in the risk of coronary disease in relation to the women who drink alcohol. So their hormone replacement therapy paper and their alcohol paper both showed about a halving of coronary risk and yet, now we've had the randomised trial with hormone replacement therapy showing no benefit and that's really what made me rethink the alcohol. And so I think that we're mixing two things up because moderate drinkers are moderate people, and moderate people do all sorts of other things in moderation which is good for your health.

What people would say is that they've controlled for those factors, you know they've looked at whether or not they take physical activity and they're thin and all that sort of thing.

Yeah, but I think that's what was, to excuse the pun, the most sobering thing for me is that the Nurses' Health Study felt that they had control when they did their hormone replacement study paper and showed a 50% reduction. They believed that they had done a very good job at controlling for confounding.[1] But clearly with the randomised trials and now there's three randomised trials, it's not just the HERS Study. So it's pretty clear now that there was uncontrolled confounding that accounted for about a halving of risk.

1. A confounding factor in scientific study is something the authors didn't consider that is the real explanation for their results.

Confounding Factors

The critics of the alcohol theory years used to say well look people who either don't drink or drink lightly are actually sicker, or there are things wrong with them and that's why they don't drink and that actually clouds the whole alcohol statistic. And you quote a recent study from the United States which suggests that in fact that indeed may be true.

Yeah, I mean people who are non-drinkers are different from drinkers. In the study I quote, there was a telephone survey which some people have poo poohed but for this kind of study it's as good as anything. A large study, 200,000 of thirty cardiovascular risk factors 90%, 27 out of 30 were more prevalent than the non-drinkers. So there really are differences between non-drinkers and drinkers. You know of course in our analyses we can only adjust for the things that we know about and I think the hormone replacement debacle has taught us that for coronary heart disease at least it's not that easy to control for things. Because coronary heart disease is such an easy disease to modify that it's very likely that there are all sorts of unknown confounders.

When you say easy to modify you mean what?

We know that within months of stopping smoking your risk of a coronary has dropped dramatically. We know that within less than a year of taking blood pressure lowering or cholesterol lowering drugs your risk has substantially declined.

In other words there are so many risk factors modifying one of them will make a difference.

Yeah, there are kind of two things. One there are a lot of risk factors that are modifiable and the other thing is that the impact of modifying them seems to happen amazingly quickly—like within a year.

Some Protective Effects

Now you don't reject the notion that alcohol may be cardio-protective?

No, I've looked at arguments on both sides, the kind of believers and non-believers and I think they both got it partly right and partly wrong. Alcohol increases your good cholesterol and reduces the stickiness of your platelets, so it should be good for your arteries. But some of the studies have shown that you know one or two drinks a week is associated with a 25% reduction in heart disease. Now that's biologically not possible, so I think it's very unlikely one or two drinks is having any impact on your cholesterol or your platelet stickiness. That's all confounding, that's the kind of moderate people but by the time you're drinking two or three drinks a day you are actually increasing your good cholesterol and you're decreasing your platelet stickiness. So it's a least palatable argument, it's all these puns coming in here, but I actually think that moderate to heavy drinking is beneficial for your coronary arteries. But the downside is huge, there's overwhelming evidence that by the time you're drinking moderately to heavily, that's three or four drinks a day or more, you're doing yourself a lot of other harms and so the harms definitely outweigh the benefits. Whereas the whole argument with light drinking was that there was this window you know, that light to moderate drinking was good for your heart but it wasn't bad for anything else. And I actually don't think it is good for your heart.

No Health Benefits Overall

So where does that leave the alcohol story?

I think where it leaves it is that there are no health benefits overall, I think that there's probably no stage where the benefits outweigh the harms.

So where does that leave the French paradox?

Well the French paradox has always been a little bit dubious. Their drinking is probably protecting their hearts because they drink moderately to heavily. But road traffic death rates in continental Europe are much higher than the United Kingdom or Scandinavia for instance.

Yes in fact I've covered an economic analysis of alcohol in France and the social costs are greater.

Yeah, they're huge. See up until now the whole argument has been kind of polarised, it's you either believe that there's a benefit or you believe that there's a harm, or believe there's no benefit. And I actually, guess what I've done really is I suggested it was probably a bit of both.

That spoil sport is called Professor Jackson who's Professor of Epidemiology in the School of Population Health at the University of Auckland.

"Drinking during this critical development period [young adulthood] may
lead to lifelong impairments in brain
function."

Drinking Impairs Youth Development

U.S. Department of Health and Human Services

In the following viewpoint the U.S. Department of Health and Human Services maintains that alcohol consumption by youth can impede development. It does this by interrupting the mastery of important life skills and by impairing brain function, says the agency. According to the author, one reason that youth are at risk is their tendency to binge drink, a pattern of drinking that is likely to cause harm. The U.S. Department of Health and Human Services is a government agency established with the goal of protecting the health of all Americans.

As you read, consider the following questions:

1. According to the study, how many young adults drank more than they should at least once in 2001–2002?

2. According to the Department of Health and Human Services, what may be a key reason for alcohol's harmful effects on the youth brain?

U.S. Department of Health and Human Services, "Young Adult Drinking," *Alcohol Alert*, no. 68, April 2006.

3. What type of policies are effective in preventing alcohol-related problems, as explained by the author?

Too often today's headlines bring news of yet another alcohol-related tragedy involving a young person—a case of fatal alcohol poisoning on a college campus or a late-night drinking-driving crash. People ages 18 to 25 often are in the news, but are they really at higher risk than anyone else for problems involving alcohol?

Some of the most important new data to emerge on young adult drinking were collected through a recent nationwide survey, the National Epidemiologic Survey on Alcohol and Related Conditions (NESARC). According to these data, in 2001–2002 about 70 percent of young adults in the United States, or about 19 million people, consumed alcohol in the year preceding the survey.

Harmful Drinking Patterns

It's not only that young people are drinking but the way they drink that puts them at such high risk for alcohol-related problems. Research consistently shows that people tend to drink the heaviest in their late teens and early to mid-twenties. Young adults are especially likely to binge drink and to drink heavily. According to NESARC data, about 46 percent of young adults (12.4 million) engaged in drinking that exceeded the recommended daily limits at least once in the past year, and 14.5 percent (3.9 million) had an average consumption that exceeded the recommended weekly limits.

Such risky drinking often leads to tragic consequences—most notably alcohol-related traffic fatalities. Thirty-two percent of drivers ages 16–20 who died in traffic crashes in 2003 had measurable alcohol in their blood, and 51 percent of drivers ages 21–24 who died tested positive for alcohol. Clearly, then, young adult drinkers pose a serious public health threat, putting themselves and others at risk.

Brain Development Studies

A series of recent studies indicates that exposure to drugs of abuse during adolescence may produce more adverse effects than exposure during adulthood in part because of the important changes occurring in the brain during adolescent development. Advances in science have now brought us to a point where researchers can use new animal models, modern brain imaging technology and other neurobehavioral assessment tools to probe the effects of alcohol, tobacco and other drugs on the developing brain and determine immediate as well as its long-term behavioral consequences.

Emerging findings from neuroimaging studies demonstrate that brain structures change during adolescence to become more specialized and efficient in their functioning. Our developmentally focused research indicates important neurocognitive disadvantages among adolescents with alcohol and drug use disorders as compared to teens without substance involvement. For example, even after three weeks of abstinence, alcohol-dependent youth display a 10% decrement in delayed memory functions. Neuropsychological testing of these youth followed up to eight years demonstrates that continued heavy drinking during adolescence is associated with diminished memory of verbal and nonverbal material, and poorer performance on tests requiring attention skills.

Sandra A. Brown, testimony before the Subcommittee on Substance Abuse and Mental Health Services, Hearing and Providing Substance Abuse Prevention and Treatment Services to Adolescents, June 15, 2004.

An Age of Exploration

Young adulthood is a stage of life marked by change and exploration. People move out of their parents' homes and into dormitories or houses with peers. They go to college, begin to work full-time, and form serious relationships. They explore their own identities and how they fit in the world. The roles of parents weaken and the influences of peers gain greater strength. Young adults are on their own for the first time, free to make their own decisions, including the decision to drink alcohol.

Young adulthood also is the time during which young people obtain the education and training they need for future careers. Mastery of these endeavors is vital to future success; problems with school and work can produce frustration and stress, which can lead to a variety of unhealthy behaviors, including increased drinking. Conversely, alcohol use during this important time of transition can impede the successful mastery of these developmental tasks, also increasing stress.

Alcohol and the Maturing Brain

Research shows that the brain continues to develop throughout adolescence and well into young adulthood. Many scientists are concerned that drinking during this critical developmental period may lead to lifelong impairments in brain function, particularly as it relates to memory, motor skills, and coordination. Young adults are particularly likely to binge drink and to suffer repeated bouts of withdrawal from alcohol. This repeated withdrawal may be a key reason for alcohol's harmful effects on the brain. . . .

A Dangerous Habit

The age when people begin drinking (especially heavy drinking) has proven to be an especially good predictor of problems with alcohol later in life. Interviews of adults consistently confirm a strong association between an early initiation of drinking and later alcohol-related problems. People who binge drink also are at higher risk for later alcohol problems. And young adults who drink heavily are at particular risk for behavioral problems and may have trouble adjusting to adult roles. . . .

Despite the fact that young adults' alcohol use is in some sense "normal," it still can be dangerous. Statistics show that illness and death among young adults primarily result from lifestyle choices and behaviors, including excessive alcohol use. Even one night of heavy drinking can have serious consequences that persist well beyond adolescence and young adulthood, such as alcohol-related car crashes, unintended pregnancies, and physical assaults leading to arrest or jail. . . .

One way to prevent alcohol-related problems—among young people or the population as a whole—is to establish policies that reduce overall alcohol consumption rates or reduce the rates of high-risk drinking. Alcohol control policies influence the availability of alcohol, the social messages about drinking that are conveyed by advertising and other marketing approaches, and the enforcement of existing alcohol laws.

> *"There appears to be absolutely no evidence whatsoever that the light or moderate consumption of alcohol by persons under the age of 21 causes ... harm."*

Moderate Drinking Does Not Impair Youth Development

David J. Hanson

In the following viewpoint David J. Hanson insists that there is no evidence that moderate alcohol consumption harms youth. He believes the existing evidence about brain damage from rats and humans is not scientifically sound enough to prove such a claim. In addition, he points out that many societies outside the United States allow light and moderate youth drinking, with no harmful results. Hanson is a professor emeritus of sociology at the State University of New York at Potsdam. He has studied and written extensively on alcohol and has provided his expertise on the subject to the U.S. and Canadian governments, and many major news organizations.

David J. Hanson, "Drinking Alcohol Damages Teenagers' Brains," *Alcohol: Problems and Solutions*, 2005. www.potsdam.edu. Copyright © 1997–2007 D. J. Hanson. All rights reserved. Reproduced by permission of the author.

As you read consider the following questions:

1. How do the processes found in rats compare to the processes in humans, in Hanson's opinion?
2. According to the author, what is the problem with the existing human evidence on teen drinking and brain damage?
3. As explained by Hanson, why might drinking with parents be "protective behavior"?

Does drinking in adolescence harm brain development? Does consuming alcohol before age 21 cause permanent brain damage? Does underage drinking retard mental development?

Warning About Alcohol

Federal agencies warn us that:

> "Research indicates that the human brain continues to develop into a person's early twenties and that exposure of the developing brain to alcohol may have long-lasting effects on intellectual capabilities."[1]

> "Exposing the brain to alcohol during this period (i.e, before age 21) may interrupt key processes of brain development" and "alcohol-induced brain damage may persist."[2]

> "The brains and bodies of teens are still developing, and alcohol use can cause learning problems."[3]

1. Center for Substance Abuse Prevention (CSAP). A Family Guide to Keeping Youth Mentally Healthy & Drug Free: Monitor Your Child's Activities - Underage Drinking, 2005. CSAP is part of the Substance and Mental Health Services Administration (SAMHSA), a part of the U.S. Department of Health and Human Services (DHHS).
2. National Institute on Alcohol Abuse and Alcoholism (NIAAA). *Alcohol Alert: Underage Drinking—A Major Public Health Challenge*, Alcohol Alert #59, April, 2003.
3. U.S. Department of Health and Human Services (HHS) and the Substance Abuse and Mental Health Services Administration (SAMSHA). National Clearinghouse for Alcohol and Drug Information. Tips for Teens: The Truth about Alcohol—Booze, Sauce, Brews, Brewskis, Hootch, Hard Stuff, Juice.

Private interest and activist groups assert that:

"Drinking before the age of 21 can cause irreversible brain damage."[4]

"There is growing evidence to suggest that alcohol use prior to age 21 impairs crucial aspects of youthful brain development"[5]

"alcohol can do long-term and irreversible damage to critical neurological development that is ongoing during the teen-age years and continues until age 20."[6]

Similarly, newspaper stories tell us:

"research indicates that the brain continues to develop until age 21, and that young brains can be irreversibly damaged by alcohol."[7]

Research "shows the human brain doesn't stop growing until about age 21 or 22, and that alcohol consumption can alter or retard that growth, including memory, and test-taking ability."[8]

Supporting Research

The evidence about teen drinking and potential brain damage comes from two sources.

(1) The first source of evidence is from lab rats that are typically given very large doses of alcohol. Large enough quantities of alcohol appear to cause brain impairment in young rats, especially if given over a long enough period of time.

4. Mothers Against Drunk Driving (MADD) national corporate web site.
5. Center on Alcohol Marketing and Youth (CAMY). The Toll of Underage Drinking: Drunk driving, alcohol dependence, risky sexual behavior and health consequences.
6. Proctor, Swayne. 21 turns 21. Join Together, July 29, 2005. (Join Together web site)
7. MacPherson, Karen. National drinking age of 21 successful, popular. Post-Gazette, July 16, 2005.
8. Meltz, Barbara F. Alcohol study says that girls are outpacing boys. Boston Globe, August 11, 2005.

Interestingly, at lower levels of consumption, the "adolescent" rats tend to be less susceptible to motor impairment and also less easily sedated than are older rats. The conclusions to be drawn from this for rats' brains and alcohol isn't clear.

A more serious problem is that rats aren't humans and many if not most processes found in rats don't apply at all to humans. For example, innumerable drugs cure diseases in rats but the vast majority of such drugs fail to do so in humans.

(2) The second source of evidence comes from humans. However, the humans who are studied are virtually always alcohol and/or drug dependent individuals. Not surprisingly, long-time alcohol abusers tend not to do as well at a variety of mental tasks as those who don't abuse alcohol.

It appears that large enough quantities of alcohol can impair brain development in rats and that it can also do the same in humans. There's no surprising news there.

"Natural Experiments"

These studies never deal with light or moderate alcohol consumption among young humans. However, "natural experiments" on drinking among young people have been going on for thousands of years around the world.

In many societies most people drink and they begin doing so in the home from a very early age. Examples familiar to most people include Italians, Jews, Greeks, Portuguese, French, Germans and Spaniards. There is neither evidence nor any reason to even suspect that members of these groups are brain impaired compared to those societies that do not permit young people to consume alcohol.

There appears to be absolutely no evidence whatsoever that the light or moderate consumption of alcohol by persons under the age of 21 causes any brain impairment or harm. Of course, that doesn't justify breaking any laws.

The European Example

The National Youth Rights Association urges an honest attempt be made to model American alcohol policy after Europe. Europeans learn how to drink moderately and responsibly. We must look to the long experience of Italians, Jews, Portuguese, Greeks, Spaniards and many other groups around the world. These groups typically consume alcohol on a regular daily basis but have very few drinking problems. . . .

These groups do not view alcohol as a dangerous poison drug to be avoided nor as a magic potion that can solve life's problems. They view it as a neutral substance that can be good or bad, depending on how it is used.

National Youth Rights Association, "Drinking Age Solutions."
www.youthrights.org.

Benefits of Supervised Drinking

Federally funded research does suggest that teens who drink alcohol with their parents are less likely than others to have either consumed alcohol or abused it in recent weeks according to a nation-wide study of over 6,200 teenagers in 242 communities across the U.S.

Drinking alcohol with parents "may help teach them responsible drinking habits or extinguish some of the 'novelty' or 'excitement' of drinking" according to senior researcher Dr. Kristie Long Foley of the School of Medicine at Wake Forest University. Dr. Foley describes drinking with parents as a "protective" behavior.

Contrary to popular belief, drinking with parental approval is legal in many states across the country. Only seven states prohibit those under age 21 from drinking under all circumstances.

Needless to say, no one of any age should ever overconsume or abuse alcohol.

| "There is no known safe amount of alcohol to drink while pregnant."

Any Alcohol Use During Pregnancy Is Harmful

Centers for Disease Control and Prevention

In the following viewpoint, the Centers for Disease Control and Prevention (CDC) maintains that any alcohol consumption during pregnancy may be harmful to the unborn baby. According to the CDC, alcohol can cause fetal alcohol spectrum disorders (FASDs) that result in lifelong physical, mental, and behavioral disabilities. These problems can be prevented simply by not drinking alcohol while pregnant, it insists. The CDC is a government agency that works to protect the health and safety of all Americans.

As you read, consider the following questions:

1. What are the reported rates of FAS, according to the author?

2. As explained by the CDC, how are secondary conditions such as criminal behavior and unemployment related to FASDs?

Centers for Disease Control and Prevention, "Fetal Alcohol Spectrum Disorders," *www.cdc.gov*, May 2, 2006.

3. How can fathers help prevent FASDs, in the opinion of the author?

When a pregnant woman drinks alcohol, so does her unborn baby. There is no known safe amount of alcohol to drink while pregnant and there also does not appear to be a safe time to drink during pregnancy either. Therefore, it is recommended that women abstain from drinking alcohol at any time during pregnancy. Women who are sexually active and do not use effective birth control should also refrain from drinking because they could become pregnant and not know for several weeks or more.

What Are FAS and FASDs?

Prenatal exposure to alcohol can cause a range of disorders, known as fetal alcohol spectrum disorders (FASDs). One of the most severe effects of drinking during pregnancy is fetal alcohol syndrome (FAS). FAS is one of the leading known preventable causes of mental retardation and birth defects. If a woman drinks alcohol during her pregnancy, her baby can be born with FAS, a lifelong condition that causes physical and mental disabilities. FAS is characterized by abnormal facial features, growth deficiencies, and central nervous system (CNS) problems. People with FAS might have problems with learning, memory, attention span, communication, vision, hearing, or a combination of these. These problems often lead to difficulties in school and problems getting along with others. FAS is a permanent condition. It affects every aspect of an individual's life and the lives of his or her family.

Fetal alcohol spectrum disorders (FASDs) is an umbrella term describing the range of effects that can occur in an individual whose mother drank alcohol during pregnancy. These effects include physical, mental, behavioral, and/or learning disabilities with possible lifelong implications. . . .

FASDs include FAS as well as other conditions in which individuals have some, but not all, of the clinical signs of FAS.

Three terms often used are fetal alcohol effects (FAE), alcohol-related neurodevelopmental disorder (ARND), and alcohol-related birth defects (ARBD). The term FAE has been used to describe behavioral and cognitive problems in children who were prenatally exposed to alcohol, but who do not have all of the typical diagnostic features of FAS. In 1996, the Institute of Medicine (IOM) replaced FAE with the terms ARND and ARBD. Children with ARND might have functional or mental problems linked to prenatal alcohol exposure. These include behavioral or cognitive abnormalities or a combination of both. Children with ARBD might have problems with the heart, kidneys, bones, and/or hearing.

All FASDs are 100% preventable—if a woman does not drink alcohol while she is pregnant.

How Common Are FAS and FASDs?

The reported rates of FAS vary widely. These different rates depend on the population studied and the surveillance methods used. CDC [Centers for Disease Control] studies show FAS rates ranging from 0.2 to 1.5 per 1,000 live births in different areas of the United States. Other FASDs are believed to occur approximately three times as often as FAS.

What Are the Characteristics of Children with FAS and Other FASDs?

FAS is the severe end of a spectrum of effects that can occur when a woman drinks during pregnancy. Fetal death is the most extreme outcome. FAS is a disorder characterized by abnormal facial features and growth and central nervous system (CNS) problems. If a pregnant women drinks alcohol but her child does not have all of the symptoms of FAS, it is possible that her child has another FASD, such as alcohol-related neurodevelopmental disorder (ARND). Children with ARND do not have full FAS but might demonstrate learning and behavioral problems caused by prenatal exposure to alcohol. Ex-

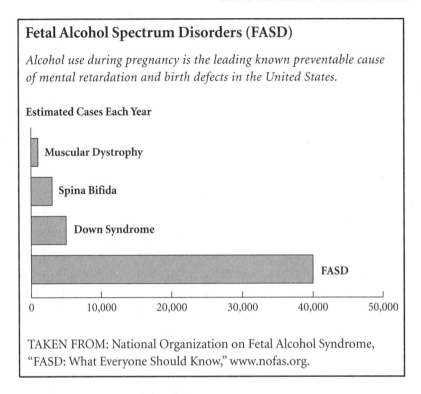

Fetal Alcohol Spectrum Disorders (FASD)

Alcohol use during pregnancy is the leading known preventable cause of mental retardation and birth defects in the United States.

Estimated Cases Each Year

Muscular Dystrophy

Spina Bifida

Down Syndrome

FASD

0   10,000   20,000   30,000   40,000   50,000

TAKEN FROM: National Organization on Fetal Alcohol Syndrome, "FASD: What Everyone Should Know," www.nofas.org.

amples of these problems are difficulties with mathematical skills, difficulties with memory or attention, poor school performance, and poor impulse control and/or judgment.

Children with FASDs might have the following characteristics or exhibit the following behaviors:

- Small size for gestational age or small stature in relation to peers

- Facial abnormalities such as small eye openings

- Poor coordination

- Hyperactive behavior

- Learning disabilities

- Developmental disabilities (e.g., speech and language delays)

- Mental retardation or low IQ

- Problems with daily living

- Poor reasoning and judgment skills

- Sleep and sucking disturbances in infancy

Secondary Conditions

Children with FASDs are at risk for psychiatric problems, criminal behavior, unemployment, and incomplete education. These are secondary conditions that an individual is not born with but might acquire as a result of FAS or a related disorder. These conditions can be very serious, but there are protective factors that have been found to help individuals with FASDs. For example, a child who is diagnosed early in life can be placed in appropriate educational classes and given access to social services that can help the child and his or her family. Children with FASDs who receive special education are more likely to achieve their developmental and educational potential. In addition, children with FASDs need a loving, nurturing, and stable home life to avoid disruptions, transient lifestyles, or harmful relationships. Children with FASDs who live in abusive or unstable homes or who become involved in youth violence are much more likely than those who do not have such negative experiences to develop secondary conditions. . . .

How Can We Prevent FASDs?

FASDs are completely preventable—if a woman does not drink alcohol while she is pregnant or could become pregnant. If a woman is drinking during pregnancy, it is never too late for her to stop. The sooner a woman stops drinking, the better it will be for both her baby and herself. If a woman is not able to stop drinking, she should contact her doctor, local Alcoholics Anonymous, or local alcohol treatment center. The Substance Abuse and Mental Health Services Administration has a

Substance Abuse Treatment Facility locator. This locator helps people find drug and alcohol treatment programs in their area. If a woman is sexually active and is not using an effective form of birth control, she should not drink alcohol. She could become pregnant and not know it for several weeks or more.

Mothers are not the only ones who can prevent FASDs. The father's role is also important in helping the mother abstain from drinking alcohol during pregnancy. He can encourage her not drinking alcohol by avoiding social situations that involve drinking and by not drinking alcohol himself. Significant others, family members, schools, health and social service organizations, and communities can also help prevent FASDs through education and intervention.

In February 2005, the U.S. Surgeon General issued an Advisory on Alcohol Use in Pregnancy to raise public awareness about this important health concern. To reduce prenatal alcohol exposure, prevention efforts should target not only pregnant women who are currently drinking, but also women who could become pregnant, are drinking at high-risk levels, and are having unprotected sex.

| *"There is no conclusive evidence to demonstrate that moderate drinking during pregnancy can harm the fetus."*

The Risks of Alcohol Consumption During Pregnancy Have Been Exaggerated

Daniel Rogov

The harms of alcohol to the unborn baby have been exaggerated, argues Daniel Rogov in the following viewpoint. While heavy consumption can cause birth defects, there is no evidence that moderate drinking is risky, says Rogov. He points out that some studies even show that it may actually be beneficial during pregnancy. In his opinion, pregnant women should not be criticized if they decide to consume a moderate amount of alcohol. Rogov is the Wine and Food Critic of HaAretz *newspaper in Israel and maintains a wine and gastronomy Internet site.*

As you read, consider the following questions:

1. According to Whitten and Lipp, as cited by Rogov, what is the occurrence of fetal alcohol syndrome?

Daniel Rogov, "Wine and Pregnancy: Lies That Women Are Told," *Women Wine Critics Board*, January 5, 2006. Reproduced by permission of the author.

2. In Rogov's opinion, what do studies since the mid-1980s show about the correlation between moderate alcohol consumption and birth defects?

3. How might moderate drinking be beneficial to pregnancy, as explained by Rogov?

Since 1990 every bottle of wine, beer and spirits sold in the United States has carried the warning that "according to the Surgeon General, women should not drink alcoholic beverages during pregnancy because of the risk of birth defects." If that has not been enough to add to the anxiety of women already concerned about their own health and the health of their fetuses, hundreds of newspaper articles and television talk shows have been devoted to convincing women that if they have even a single drink during their pregnancy that there is a chance that their baby will be born deformed, addicted to alcohol or retarded.

An Exaggerated Risk

It seems, however, as if the American government, medical authorities and media have not been telling American women the entire truth. Although the official message is "don't drink at all during pregnancy", a great deal of recent research and a re-examination of the alcohol-pregnancy issue show that there is no conclusive evidence to demonstrate that moderate drinking during pregnancy can harm the fetus.

According to doctors David Whitten and Martin Lipp of the University of California at San Francisco, "the campaign against drinking during pregnancy started in 1973 when several studies showed that heavy drinking during pregnancy can cause the condition known as the Fetal Alcohol Syndrome." These studies demonstrated that the children of many alcoholic mothers were born with a cluster of severe birth defects. "What the government conveniently chose to ignore," say Whitten and Lipp, "is that this syndrome is extremely rare, oc-

Total Abstinence Not Necessary

Medical evidence suggests that, as long as you drink no more than one or two units of alcohol, once or twice a week, and avoid getting drunk, it is unlikely that your baby will be affected.

These are the NHS [National Health Service of the United Kingdom] recommended maximum allowances:

- ordinarily, women can drink up to 2 to 3 units of alcohol a day

- pregnant women can drink up to 1 to 2 units of alcohol no more than once or twice a week

National Health Service,
"How Much Is Too Much When You're Having a Baby," 2006.
www.dh.gov.uk.

curring only 3 times in 100,000 births, and then only when the mother drinks abusively throughout her pregnancy."

Lipp and Whitten, whose "To Your Health" was published in 1995, are among an increasing number of doctors and researchers who feel that pregnant women have no reason to fear drinking a glass of wine every day. As revealed by contributing editor Thomas Matthews in the August 31, 1994 issue of the "Wine Spectator" magazine which was devoted largely to this controversy, "there is even new research that shows that moderate drinking during pregnancy may actually help the development of the child after birth."

An Unjustified Argument

No one questions the fact that the consumption of large amounts of alcohol during pregnancy can harm the fetus. It has been well established, for example, that the children of women who drink more than 3–4 glasses of wine daily show significant decreases in birth weight and length than those of women who drink 1–2 glasses daily, and it is generally accepted that having five or more drinks per day is especially dangerous to the fetus. Here, however, agreement ends, and Genevieve Knupfer of the Alcohol Research Group in Berkeley, California says that part of the problem comes about because many of the studies that reported adverse effects on the fetus used imprecise methodology. In several studies, for example, researchers arbitrarily defined "heavy drinkers" as those women who consumed more than one glass of wine daily.

Feeling even more strongly, Dr. Michael Samuels of New York City's Doctor's Hospital says that the data has been "turned around for the purpose of frightening women," and indicates that birth defects of any kind occur in 3–5% of babies born in the United States and only 1–2% of those can be related to the ingestion of alcohol. Based on the data of Samuels and other medical researchers, it becomes clear that less than 0.1% of all birth defects are related to alcohol, and that more than 90% of the affected children are born to women with a history of alcohol abuse.

More than this, not even one study carried out since the mid-1980s has shown a direct correlation between moderate alcohol consumption and birth defects. One study, of 33,300 California women showed that even though 47% drank moderately during their pregnancies that none of their babies met the criteria for Fetal Alcoholic Syndrome. The authors of this study concluded "that alcohol at moderate levels is not a significant cause of malformation in our society and that the position that moderate consumption is dangerous, is completely unjustified."

Moderate Drinking May Be Beneficial

Some studies go as far as to indicate that light to moderate drinking may actually improve the chance of successful pregnancies. A 1993 study published in the "American Journal of

Epidemiology" by Ruth Little and Clarence Weinberg concluded, for example, that there were fewer stillbirths and fewer losses of fetus due to early labor among women who consumed a moderate level of alcohol. That some alcohol can be protective against preterm birth is also supported by Dr. Martha Direnfeld of Haifa University who points out that when used properly, alcohol is known to stop unwanted uterine contractions, and thus has "saved many pregnancies that might otherwise have spontaneously aborted." More than this, Dr. Robert Sokol of the National Institute on Alcohol Abuse in Detroit has shown that it is light drinkers and not abstainers who have the best chance of having a baby of optimal birth weight, and in their book *Alcohol and the Fetus* and doctors Henry Rosset and Lynn Wiener have presented data that show that children of moderate drinkers tend to score highest on developmental tests at the age of 18 months.

Lecturing Pregnant Women

Despite these and many other findings the United States government, the American Medical Association, the British Medical Association and the vast majority of American and English doctors continue to recommend complete abstention from wine, beer and spirits during pregnancy. An examination of why this is true reveals that the issue is as emotional, ideological and political as it is medical. Well-respected wine writer Janis Robinson has declared that "in this our male dominated society, men feel entitled to lecture pregnant women on how they should best discharge their responsibilities to their unborn children." In a similar tone, Katha Pollit, writing in "The Nation" claimed that "all of these warnings allow the government to appear to be concerned about babies without having to spend any money, change any priorities or challenge any vested interests."

No one argues that there are no risks whatever in alcohol consumption during pregnancy, even at sensible levels, but as

Thomas Matthews stated in the "Wine Spectator," "it is important to ask: risky when compared to what?" In her recently published book *The Myths of Motherhood*, Shary Turner indicates that alcohol is far from the only risk factor pregnant women are warned against. Other items on the list include caffeine, chocolate, raw oysters, unpasteurized cheese, tropical fruits, drugs that alleviate cold symptoms, nail polish, suntan lotion and hair dye, all of which in some amount may harm the fetus. Turner's conclusion is that "the only risk free pregnancy is one that is meant less to benefit the baby than to imprison the mother in anxiety and self-reproach."

Women Should Choose for Themselves

In the absence of 100% certainty about the issue, many continue to insist that abstinence is the best advice to give pregnant women. Others, however, see this attitude as illogical and have concluded that the risks and benefits associated with light to moderate regular wine consumption compare quite favorably with most other activities of daily life. Doctors Whitten and Lipp write that "light, regular wine consumption, or one or two glasses of table wine per day can be part of the healthy lifestyle for most people, including pregnant women." Israeli gynecologist-researchers Howard Carp and Martha Direnfeld also feel that women who were drinking healthfully before pregnancy are not putting their fetuses in danger if they go on drinking in the same way during pregnancy. Dr. Carp states that "an occasional glass of wine or any other drink is fine, no problem at all, and those women who drink a glass of wine once or twice a week with their meals should not feel any guilt or fear at all." Like Dr. Carp, Dr. Direnfeld acknowledges the harm of drinking in excess but feels that "a reasonable amount of alcohol, say a glass of wine per day, will not harm the baby."

It is true that all of the evidence has not yet been gathered, but it is difficult not to see the logic of the conclusion that when it comes to drinking, evidence demands interpretations and decisions require judgment. Women are capable of choosing for themselves.

Periodical Bibliography

The following articles have been selected to supplement the diverse views presented in this chapter.

Atlantic Monthly	"Booze and Consequences," April 2005.
Phyllida Brown	"Sobering News for Pregnant Women," *New Scientist*, June 29, 2006.
Nancy Clark	"The Quick and the Drunk," *American Fitness*, March–April 2005.
Larry Gierer	"Pregnant Drinking Not Worth the Risk," *Columbus Ledger-Enquirer*, October 2006.
USA Today	"How Often You Drink, Not What, Cuts Heart Problems," January 8, 2003.
Thomas H. Lee	"How to Help Your Heart," *Newsweek*, April 2007.
Alan Mozes	"Binge Drinking May Be Biggest Alcohol Threat," *HealthDay*, January 2007.
Steven Reinberg	"Experts Dispute 'Healthy Drinking' Theory," *HealthDay News*, December 1, 2005.
Sarah Robbins	"Can Alcohol Boost Brain Power?" *Shape*, August 2006.
T. Santibanez, L. Barker, J. Santoll, et al.,	"Alcohol-Attributable Deaths and Years of Potential Life Lost—United States, 2001," *Morbidity and Mortality Weekly Report*, September 24, 2004.
Anne Underwood	"A Health Toast," *Newsweek*, October 3, 2005.
U.S. Department of Heath and Human Services	"Alcohol's Damaging Effects on the Brain," *Alcohol Alert*, October 2004.
Hillary Wright	"To Drink or Not to Drink? The Pros and Cons of Imbibing Alcohol," *Environmental Nutrition*, March 2006.

OPPOSING
VIEWPOINTS®
SERIES

CHAPTER 2

Is Alcohol Use Harmful to Society?

Chapter Preface

In a 2007 press conference, Koren Zailckas, author of *Smashed: Story of a Drunken Girlhood*, tells the story of her drinking experiences in youth. Zailckas had her first drink when she was fourteen. She drank throughout high school, and at age sixteen needed to have her stomach pumped to save her from alcohol poisoning, but she continued to drink heavily throughout college. While she believes her experience was fairly typical of many young girls, Zailckas also believes it was extremely harmful. She says, "I saw some of those more horrifying consequences that result from this kind of under-age drinking and binge drinking—a lot of alcohol-fueled depression, a lot of blackouts, things like date rape and sexual assaults." Because alcohol use is so widespread, this drug affects many parts of society. As Zailckas' story illustrates, girls—who are drinking more than in years past—constitute one group that seems to be increasingly affected by alcohol.

Research shows that girls are starting to drink at younger ages and are consuming significantly more alcohol than in the past. The New York State Office of Alcoholism and Substance Abuse Services reports: "Girls' behavior concerning alcohol has changed over the past 20 years. Girls today are four times more likely to begin drinking before age 16 than their mothers were." Statistics show that girls are catching up to, and even surpassing, the drinking rates of boys. For example, in 2004 the Substance Abuse and Mental Health Services Administration found that 18 percent of girls reported drinking alcohol in the past month, compared to 17.2 percent of boys. Overall, the agency finds that 1,500,000 teenage girls started using alcohol that year.

Many people argue that this increased alcohol use is having various harmful effects on girls. According to Joseph Califano, president of the National Center on Addiction and Substance Abuse at Columbia University in New York, one drink for a teenage girl has about the same impact as two drinks for a teenage boy because of differences between male and female metabolism and body weight. The Office of National Drug Control Policy insists that increased alcohol use by girls is related to numerous problems. For example, it states, "Adolescent girls who consume even moderate amounts of alcohol may experience disrupted growth and puberty." According to the organization, girls who drink alcohol are also more likely to have unplanned and unprotected sex. It reports that in a study of unplanned pregnancies among fourteen- to twenty-one-year-olds, one third of the girls had been drinking when they had sex and became pregnant.

Critics of these organizations believe that the prevalence of alcohol use by girls, and its associated problems, have been exaggerated. They point out that even if alcohol consumption among girls has increased, it still only takes place among a minority of youth. For example, according to the 2005 Monitoring the Future Survey of American Teenagers, binge drinking among high-school age youth has decreased and the number of youth who believe such behavior is risky has increased. Critics also argue that the statistics on girls' drinking may be misleading because more girls are admitting to drinking than in the past.

Girls are not the only segment of society affected by alcohol consumption. Alcohol is widely consumed and has far-reaching effects. As the following chapter reveals, however, there is disagreement over whether these effects are beneficial or harmful to society.

| *"Alcohol abuse costs American businesses an estimated $134 billion a year."*

The Economy Is Harmed by Alcohol

Susan Brink

Alcohol abuse costs the American economy billions of dollars a year says Susan Brink in the following viewpoint. According to Brink, a large number of Americans have drinking problems that interfere with their work and cause accidents and lower productivity; however, the majority of these people do not receive adequate treatment. Brink believes that businesses should invest in providing treatment for employees with alcohol problems. She is a contributing writer for U.S. News & World Report.

As you read, consider the following questions:

1. As stated by Brink, how much sick leave do people with untreated alcohol problems use compared to other employees?

2. According to the author, in a corporation with 10,000 workers, approximately how many will have alcohol problems?

3. How much does alcohol abuse add to the nation's annual medical tab, according to Brink?

Lynn Cooper knew it as she stood in the glow of the refrigerator light against the early evening darkness. She knew it as the warmth of her house penetrated her winter coat and hat, knew it as she reached for the wine bottle in her still-gloved, trembling hand. She knew—as she greedily poured the first of the evening's multiple glasses of wine—that she had a serious drinking problem. "I was standing there with a full glass of wine in my hand," she recalls, "and I hadn't even taken my gloves off."

Costs of Alcohol Abuse

When she had her epiphany 14 years ago, she was a company vice president. She supervised a large staff. She made a lot of money. As she says, "I was a functional alcoholic."

But often, particularly on Mondays, she didn't function well at all. She'd wake up late, her head pounding, her guts roiling, and she'd call in sick. Today, she seldom misses a day of work. But she still recalls that when she was drinking, the 15 annual sick days she had coming were never near enough to cover the leave she needed for hangovers.

Alcohol abuse costs American businesses an estimated $134 billion a year. People with untreated alcohol problems use twice as much sick leave as other employees. They have more on-the-job accidents. They are five times as likely to file a workers' compensation claim.

Addiction research is steadily making progress in identifying the kinds of treatment programs that work for people with a variety of drinking problems. But unhappily, the accumulating scientific evidence on treatment effectiveness rarely translates into appropriate insurance coverage for such addictions. Indeed, addiction coverage typically has caps on both dollar reimbursement and time in treatment. What's more, patients, when they get treatment at all, are often steered into one-size-fits-all programs that don't fit the majority of those in need.

Lack of Treatment

When it comes to treatment for alcohol problems, geography rules. A study by Eric Goplerud of the George Washington University Medical Center found that only seven states require alcohol treatment to be covered at the same level as diabetes, heart disease, and other life-threatening illnesses. And although addicts in those states are more likely to get the treatment they need, even there the mandates are often ignored. Eighteen states have limits on coverage for alcohol problems. In Texas, for example, coverage is required for three "episodes" in a lifetime. Arkansas law sets a lifetime figure of $12,000 for alcohol treatment, and Ohio mandates $550 a year. In much of the country, "insurance either doesn't cover the treatment, or it doesn't cover the right things, or it doesn't cover enough of it," says Goplerud.

Cooper was lucky. Her insurance covered a form of treatment that allowed her to keep working. She never went into a residential treatment program—the type that can keep someone off the job and away from home for 28 days or more. "I was in a 90-day treatment program. I would work until 4 o'clock, then go for treatment from 5 to 9, four days a week. After the first month, it was two days a week," she says. And while Alcoholics Anonymous [AA] has been a successful support group for millions, she found meetings with Women For Sobriety to be a better match for her after treatment. "I'm here to tell you that if all they offered me was a 28-day program and AA, I'd still be drinking," says the 48-year-old Cooper. She now represents drug and alcohol treatment providers at the Pennsylvania Community Providers Association in Harrisburg, Pa.

Cost of Underage and Pathological Drinking

Analysis of the most recently available relevant data . . . reveals that the alcohol industry depends on underage and pathological . . . drinking for a minimum of $48.3 billion or 37.5 percent of total consumer expenditures for its products and as much as $62.9 billion or 48.8 percent. . . .

If unchecked, the alcohol industry stands to gain at least one-half trillion dollars in cash revenues over the next decade from product sales to underage and pathological drinkers. This represents a profound conflict of interest with the public health.

Alcohol abuse and alcoholism cost the nation an estimated $220 billion in 2005, more than cancer ($196 billion) or obesity ($133 billion). Because of the high price Americans pay in dollars and human suffering, the U.S. Department of Health and Human Services has identified the reduction of underage drinking and abusive and dependent—pathological—drinking a priority national health objective in the United States in its *Healthy People 2010* report.

National Center on Addiction and Substance Abuse at Columbia University, "The Commercial Value of Underage and Pathological Drinking to the Alcohol Industry," May 2006. www.casacolumbia.org.

The treatment program that worked for Cooper is just one of those described by the American Society of Addict Medicine [ASAM]. But the problem is that few people have access to such individualized care. "We know a lot about what works," says Michael Flaherty, executive director of the Institute for Research, Education and Training in Addictions, in Pittsburgh. "The science is 10 years ahead of practice and 15 years ahead of most policy."

Everybody's Different

Treatment needs vary greatly. Some people need residential treatment for a month or so. Others could benefit from simply using their two weeks of vacation leave for residential treatment, then continuing with outpatient treatment. Still others need less frequent but longer-term outpatient treatment. New medications like the FDA [Food and Drug Administration]-approved naltrexone and Acamprosate (not yet approved by the agency)[1] can help some drinkers by targeting pathways in the brain and blocking the high that alcoholics seek. Some adults, and almost all adolescents, need social or psychiatric services as well. Women often need child care and generally do better in female-only treatment programs. And almost everyone has family members who need professional guidance in sorting out the tangle of issues that come with loving an addict.

Employers who purchase insurance plans typically don't buy coverage for all the options. And their workplaces reflect the nation's drinking problems. For example, a corporation with 10,000 workers will have an average of 600 employees with alcohol problems. Of those, 30 will receive treatment in a given year, and 22 will be employable a year later. But a company's human resources department could choose differently. It could pay the insurance company to provide outreach services, which would identify twice as many problem drinkers and encourage them to seek treatment. The net result for the company would be 40 employees still on the job a year later. "We know the relationship between amount of services and aftercare and outcomes. We know if we want 40 of 60 people employable, [insurers] have to fund six months of aftercare," says psychologist Norman Hoffmann of Brown University. Hoffmann helped develop widely used criteria for diagnosis and treatment of alcoholism. Unfortunately, few employers are even aware of the variety of treatment options

1. Acamprosate was approved in 2004.

they should be shopping for when choosing an insurer, says David Mee-Lee, chair of ASAM and editor of the organization's treatment guidelines.

Accounting

The cruel irony is that despite the high cost of alcohol abuse to businesses, it isn't always in the financial interest of an employer to cover addiction treatment. "Employee replacement costs can vary from $25 to $150,000," says Hoffman. "If it's going to cost you $150,000 to replace somebody who runs a train or fixes an airplane, you can afford to spend some money to keep that person well and on the job." But a fast-food chain could replace an alcoholic worker for the cost of a newspaper ad.

Ironically, the medical consequences associated with heavy drinking, such as cancer, stroke, cirrhosis of the liver, and injuries from falls and traffic accidents, are all typically covered by insurance. Indeed, alcohol abuse adds $23 billion to the nation's annual medical tab. When Cooper was drinking heavily, she underwent a brain scan as physicians tried to figure out why she had chronic headaches. She also had numerous tests to unravel the medical mystery of her gastrointestinal disorders. And she fell on several occasions, sometimes requiring medical treatment. At the peak of her drinking, she was downing several bottles of wine a day. Not coincidentally, she says, "My medical file was 8 inches thick."

"*The beer industry in the U.S. spends $1.36 billion in advertising annually, employs 1.78 million people and pays $54 billion in wages and benefits.*"

The Economy Benefits from Alcohol

Bill Reed

In the following viewpoint Bill Reed points out that while alcohol does have negative effects on society, it also has a beneficial impact on the economy. For example, he says, the beer industry employs more than a million people, pays billions of dollars in taxes, and invests billions in advertising. In his opinion, the challenge is to enjoy these economic benefits while limiting alcohol-related problems. Reed is a journalist for the Colorado Springs Gazette.

As you read, consider the following questions:

1. What does the Beer Institute say about government estimates of the costs of alcohol, as cited by Reed?

2. According to the author, how much do beer sales contribute to taxes every year?

3. In Reed's opinion, how has alcohol contributed to Tejon Street in the city of Colorado Springs?

Is alcohol really such a drain on our pocketbooks? What about taxes collected from the sale of alcohol, and the jobs created by the alcohol industry, and the health benefits of wine?

Disagreement on the Costs of Alcohol

Some argue that government estimates of the costs of alcohol are voodoo economics. Among this camp—led by voices such as Gene Ford, author of *The Science of Healthy Drinking*, and the beer industry—the favorite study cited pegs the costs of alcohol at only $12 billion annually. In government studies, the cost of motor vehicle crashes alone is higher than that.

The Beer Institute (a lobbyist for the beer industry) and others say estimates of costs are grossly exaggerated and that estimates ignore the benefits of alcohol.

The "lost productivity" figures in the National Institute on Alcohol Abuse and Alcoholism [NIAAA] estimate are the main source of contention, and that number accounts for more than half of the NIAAA's $185 billion estimate. Writers such as Ford say "lost productivity" is a ridiculous category.

Most independent academic researchers side with the NIAAA's methodology in creating estimates of the cost of alcohol abuse. NIAAA officials say the bulk of complaints they receive say the estimate is too conservative.

Nevertheless, alcohol isn't, all bad.

Economic Contributions

Nationally, beer sales alone pull in $30 billion in taxes, according to the Beer Institute. The beer industry in the U.S. spends $1.36 billion in advertising annually, employs 1.78 million people and pays $54 billion in wages and benefits. (The beer industry accounts for 85 percent of the total U.S. alcohol industry, according to *Food and Drink Weekly*.)

A Valued Part of the Community

Employees ... value the brewing sector, as one with relatively high productivity per employee and therefore good conditions in terms of wages and other labour conditions. Brewing companies are also very active in local communities, supporting many clubs and events, and on a national and global level through the sponsorship of major sports competitions and clubs. Brewers also take their social responsibility very seriously, contributing, through financing and other support, to campaigns to tackle drunk driving and other forms of misuse of their products.

Ernst & Young,
"The Contribution Made by Beer to the European Economy,"
January 2006.

Even locally, costs can be confusing. The cost of alcohol is clear at the Memorial Hospital emergency room, or the scene of a traffic fatality caused by a drunken driver.

But the downtown strip of Tejon Street was revitalized, in part, by bars and nightclubs that survive on alcohol sales.

There are 744 liquor licenses issued in the city of Colorado Springs, mostly for hotels and restaurants (343), off-premises 3.2 percent beer licenses (134), liquor stores (118) and taverns (98). Those 744 licenses represent thousands of local jobs.

Costs Versus Benefits

Is that benefit offset by the cost of extra police officers, more drunken drivers and more fights, or is it a wash? Do only beer producers and bar owners benefit, while the rest of society pays? Apparently, no one has done a "general equilibrium model," as economists call it, to weigh these costs against benefits.

But when you add up wages from the alcohol industry, taxes collected and protective benefits for the heart of moderate drinking, the ledger could be even.

The challenge, then, is to enjoy the benefits of alcohol sales to the economy while limiting the costs of alcohol abuse.

How do we have our beer and drink it, too?

> "*[There is] a strong association between alcohol consumption and an increase in individuals' risks of being a perpetrator of violence and a victim of violence.*"

Alcohol Consumption Is Linked to Violence

World Health Organization

As the World Health Organization (WHO) states in the following viewpoint, there is a strong link between alcohol consumption and violence. Research shows that a high percentage of both perpetrators and victims of violence have consumed alcohol prior to the violent incident, says WHO, and that alcohol-related violence affects both men and women and people across all age groups. The organization believes that such violence is harmful to communities and must not be tolerated. WHO, an agency of the United Nations, works to improve the health of people all over the world.

As you read, consider the following questions:

1. According to WHO, how do alcohol's effects on cognitive and physical functioning contribute to violence?

2. In the author's opinion, how do a person's beliefs about the effects of alcohol influence alcohol-related violence?

3. According to the author, how does alocohol-related violence contribute to other health and crime issues?

A cross Europe, alcohol and interpersonal violence continue to challenge public health, placing huge burdens on communities and individuals as well as health, judicial and other public services. The European Region of the World Health Organization (WHO) has the highest per capita levels of alcohol consumption in the world. Alcohol is responsible for between 6.8% (western Europe) and 12.1% (eastern Europe) of all years of health lost through premature death or disability (based on disability-adjusted life years [DALYs]). Interpersonal violence ... is responsible for about 73,000 deaths per year in the European Region, almost 1% of total deaths. For every death caused through interpersonal violence, a further 20–40 victims require hospital treatment, with many more remaining untreated and unrecorded. There is great variation in death rates from interpersonal violence throughout the region. When taken together people living in the low to middle income countries of the region are almost 14 times more likely to die from this cause than those living in high income countries. Drinking patterns and levels of interpersonal violence (such as homicide) vary widely throughout Europe. However, across all cultures they are strongly linked. Each affects and exacerbates the effects of the other ... with a strong association between alcohol consumption and an increase in individuals' risks of being a perpetrator of violence and a victim of violence.

Link Between Alcohol and Violence

Numerous mechanisms link alcohol and interpersonal violence.

- Alcohol use directly affects cognitive and physical functioning. Reduced self-control and ability to process incoming information makes drinkers more likely to resort to violence in confrontation (for example, youth violence), and reduced ability to recognize warning signs in potentially violent situations makes them appear to be easy targets for perpetrators (for example, sexual violence).

- Individual and societal beliefs that alcohol causes aggressive behaviour can lead to the use of alcohol as a way of excusing violent acts (for example, intimate partner violence).

- Dependence on alcohol means that individuals may fail to fulfil care responsibilities or extort money from relatives to purchase alcohol (for example, abuse of elderly people).

- Experiencing or witnessing violence can lead to the use of alcohol as a way of coping or self-medicating (for example, as a consequence of child abuse).

- Uncomfortable, crowded and poorly managed drinking settings contribute to increased aggression among drinkers (for example, youth violence).

- Alcohol and violence may be related through a common risk factor (for example, antisocial personality disorder) that contributes to the risk of both heavy drinking and violent behaviour.

- Prenatal alcohol exposure (resulting in fetal alcohol syndrome or fetal alcohol effects) is associated with behavioural and social problems, including delinquent behaviour, sexual violence and suicide in later life. . . .

The involvement of alcohol in violence is not routinely recorded across Europe in either health or criminal justice settings, and many incidents of violence remain unreported to authorities and hence undetected. However, across all industrialized countries (including countries in the WHO European Region), alcohol is estimated to be responsible for 41% of male and 32% of female DALYs lost through homicide. Nevertheless, such figures mask cultural variation, and links between alcohol and violence appear to be stronger in countries where drinking is characterized by acute intoxication.

Across all of Europe, health and criminal justice studies increasingly highlight the role of alcohol consumption in people becoming victims of violence and perpetrators of violence. Key findings include the following.

Alcohol Consumption by Perpetrators and Victims of Violence

- Among victims of assaults presenting at an emergency department in Norway, 53% assessed that their attacker had consumed alcohol prior to the attack.

- In the Russian Federation, almost 75% of individuals arrested for homicide in 1995 had consumed alcohol.

- In England and Wales, national survey data (2003–2004) showed that perpetrators of violence had been drinking in half (50%) of all violent incidents, equivalent to more than 1.3 million incidents of alcohol-related violence per year.

- Among victims of homicide 15–64 years old in Finland (1987–1996), 62.7% of men and 36.8% of women tested positive for alcohol.

- In the Netherlands (1970–1998), 36% of patients presenting to a hospital trauma centre with injuries sustained through violence had consumed alcohol versus 6.6% of patients attending with accidental injuries.

- In Spain, 36% of patients attending an emergency department with violence-related injuries had consumed alcohol in the six hours prior to injury.

A Key Factor in Interpersonal Violence

Alcohol is a key factor across all types of interpersonal violence. European studies have shown the following.

Alcohol and youth violence

Among men 18–24 years old in England and Wales, those who binge drink (having felt very drunk at least monthly during the past 12 months) are more than twice as likely to have committed a violent crime in the previous year as regular but non-binge drinkers. In Estonia, 80% of violent crime committed by youths has been linked to alcohol. In Norway, violent behaviour among 12- to 20-year-olds has been associated with having friends who regularly drink alcohol and having parents who are often intoxicated.

Alcohol and child abuse

Among schoolchildren aged 10-14 years in Latvia, Lithuania and the former Yugoslav Republic of Macedonia, overuse of alcohol by parents was significantly associated with emotional and physical abuse and correlated at a lower rate in the Republic of Moldova. In Germany, 32% of the offenders in cases of fatal child abuse (1985–1990) were thought to have consumed alcohol before committing the offence.

Drinking and Violence in U.S. Colleges

- **Assault**: More than 696,000 students between the ages of 18 and 24 are assaulted by another student who has been drinking. . . .

- **Vandalism**: About 11 percent of college student drinkers report that they have damaged property while under the influence of alcohol.

- **Property Damage**: More than 25 percent of administrators from schools with relatively low drinking levels and over 50 percent from schools with high drinking levels say their campuses have a "moderate" or "major" problem with alcohol-related property damage.

- **Police Involvement**: About 5 percent of 4-year college students are involved with the police or campus security as a result of their drinking and an estimated 110,000 students between the ages of 18 and 24 are arrested for an alcohol-related violation such as public drunkenness or driving under the influence.

College Drinking Prevention,
"A Snapshot of Annual High-Risk College Drinking Consequences,"
September 23, 2005. www.collegedrinkingprevention.gov.

Alcohol and intimate partner violence

In Switzerland, 33% of perpetrators and 9.5% of victims of intimate partner violence were intoxicated at the time of the event. A study of domestic abuse of pregnant women in Malta found that both victimization and perpetration were associated with alcohol consumption. In Iceland, 71% of the female victims of intimate partner violence stated partner alcohol use as the main cause of their assault; and 22% reported using alcohol themselves as a coping mechanism.

Alcohol and abuse of elderly people

In England, 45% of caregivers for elderly people receiving respite care admitted to committing some form of abuse, with caregiver alcohol consumption being the most significant risk factor for physical abuse.

Alcohol and sexual violence

In Norway, early initiation to alcohol and high alcohol consumption have been associated with increased risk of sexual victimization among teenage girls, and 40% of rape victims reported consuming alcohol before the attack. In the United Kingdom, 58% of men imprisoned for rape reported having consumed alcohol in the six hours preceding the offence, and 37% were considered to be alcohol dependent. In Sweden, a previous diagnosis of alcohol dependence among sex offenders doubled the rate of reconviction for sexual violence. . . .

Risk Factors for Victims

Age, gender and drinking patterns are important risk factors for alcohol-related victimization. The risk of becoming a victim of alcohol-related assault is highest among young people (for example, 16–29 years old in England and Wales and 15–24 years old in Norway), whereas slightly older populations have a greater risk of alcohol-related homicide (for example, 25–44 years old in Finland). Emergency treatment studies consistently find that victims of alcohol-related violence are more likely to be male (for example, 80% of victims of alcohol-related assault in England and a male-female ratio of 8:7 among victims of alcohol-related violence in the Netherlands). Further, across Europe relationship between alcohol consumption and homicide rates is stronger among men than among women, with men being more likely when drinking to display aggression towards other men than towards women. However, the gender discrepancy varies with the type of violence; for alcohol-related intimate partner violence, women are at far greater risk of becoming a victim. Early initiation into alcohol use has been associated with increased risk of sexual victimization in adolescence, and experiencing sexual abuse in childhood has been associated with greater risk of alcohol dependence in later life. Greater risks of victimization have also been found among people who drink frequently, drink in greater quantities, are single, separated or divorced and who are unemployed.

Risk Factors for Perpetrators

Men commit most alcohol-related violence (for example, Norway and England and Wales), with the risk of perpetration varying with age. In the United Kingdom, those aged 16–24 years are most likely to perpetrate alcohol-related violence towards strangers, whereas people 25 years or older commit most alcohol-related violence towards acquaintances. Heavier and more frequent drinkers are more at risk, as are those who start drinking alcohol at an earlier age. The relationship between alcohol and violence is mediated by certain personality traits such as impulsiveness and anger, which increase the risk of a person becoming more aggressive after drinking. A person's beliefs about the effects of alcohol also influence the risk of committing alcohol-related violence, with a higher rate of alcohol-related aggression among people who expect alcohol consumption to increase aggression. Additional risk factors may be important for specific types of violence; for abuse of elderly people, mental health problems and financial difficulties can also increase the risk of perpetration. . . .

Effects and Costs

The consequences of alcohol-related violence are far-reaching and include physical, mental and sexual injury for victims, emotional harm and burden of care for family and friends of victims, fear of crime among the wider community and increased strain on public services. . . . Further, emergency department studies have found associations between levels of alcohol consumption by victims and perpetrators and the severity of injury. In serious assaults, alcohol may play a role in determining victims' survival, for example by reducing ability to seek urgent health care assistance or reducing perceptions of the seriousness of injury. In many countries, much alcohol-related violence occurs in and around drinking venues where drinking paraphernalia (such as glasses and bottles) are frequently used as weapons. Such assaults often lead to serious and permanent facial injury as well as emotional difficulties such as post-traumatic stress disorder.

Victims of alcohol-related assault also report emotional consequences (75% in England and Wales), and with most such violence affecting young people, the physical and mental effects result in a disproportionate loss of healthy years of life. Further, the longterm effects of experiencing alcohol-related violence, especially when alcohol is used as a way of coping with violent experiences, may include more severe mental problems such as attempted suicide. . . .

Different types of violence also carry additional consequences for victims. Alcohol-related intimate partner violence can lead to the breakdown of family relationships, with children witnessing violence between parents potentially developing substance use problems and becoming perpetrators of violence themselves in later life. For elderly people being abused, extortion of money by their alcohol-using children can lead to financial difficulties, while criminal sanctions imposed as a result of alcohol-related youth violence can reduce young people's educational and career prospects. The burden of alcohol-related violence on the provision of public services can be immense. For health and criminal justice agencies, tackling and treating the offenders and victims of alcohol-related violence is not only financially costly but also diverts resources from other health and crime issues. For wider communities, a high prevalence of alcohol-related violence increases the fear of crime and inhibits people from visiting city centres and other places associated with disorder. In addition to reducing the quality of life, these effects also reduce community cohesion, disrupt trade for local businesses and hamper cultural and social development.

Prevention

Throughout much of the WHO European Region, consuming alcohol is a normal and acceptable part of society and culture. Nevertheless, violence associated with alcohol (and consequently alcohol consumption associated with violence) poses a very important and dramatic problem that can be prevented. Central to this is creating cultural and societal environments that discourage risky drinking behaviour and do not allow alcohol to be used as an excuse for violence.

"The vast majority of drinking episodes does not lead to violence, and most violence does not involve drinking."

Most Alcohol Consumption Does Not Cause Violence

International Center for Alcohol Policies

While research does show an association between alcohol consumption and violence, there is no evidence that drinking actually causes violence, maintains the International Center for Alcohol Policies (ICAP) in the following viewpoint. In the opinion of ICAP, in most cases alcohol consumption does not lead to violence. It argues that even when violence and alcohol use occur together this does not necessarily mean that the alcohol is to blame for the violent behavior. The organization asserts that more attention should be paid to other factors that can influence both alcohol use and violence. ICAP promotes understanding of the role of alcohol in society and works to reduce the abuse of alcohol worldwide.

International Center for Alcohol Policies, (with major contribution from Helen White). "Module 7: Drinking and Violence," *ICAP Blue Book: Practical Guides for Alcohol Policy and Prevention Approaches*. Washington, DC: International Center for Alcohol Policies, April 15, 2005. Reproduced by permission.

As you read, consider the following questions:

1. As argued by the author, while alcohol consumption may be reported at the time of an offense, why does this not prove that it caused the offense?

2. According to ICAP, what is the underlying assumption of the model suggesting that violent behavior leads to heavy alcohol use?

3. How common is violence in cultures where excessive drinking and acute intoxication are common, as argued by the author?

Violence has many and complex causes. Individual, community, cultural, biological, and psychosocial factors all play significant and interactive roles. Research evidence supports an association between certain drinking patterns and some forms of violence, although there is no evidence that alcohol consumption causes violence.

No Evidence of Causality

The vast majority of drinking episodes does not lead to violence, and most violence does not involve drinking. At the same time, in the case of some individuals and groups, behavioral patterns may include both abusive alcohol consumption and violent tendencies. Currently [as of 2005], there is no simple theoretical model that adequately explains the relationship between alcohol and violence.

While there is evidence that alcohol may be involved when offenses are committed, there is no evidence that it is the cause of violence. Where alcohol consumption is reported at the time an offense is committed, this may reflect only that offenders or victims consume alcohol often, not that its consumption caused the perpetrator to commit the violent act. Another aspect that needs to be considered is that a large number of violent acts are committed in areas where it is more likely that individuals will have consumed alcohol—for example, around bars and nightclubs.

In general, higher rates of drinking, heavy drinking, and alcohol abuse are reported for violent offenders than for the general population. Alcohol abuse is also associated with intimate partner violence (IPV), sexual assaults, and suicide. Further, IPV is perpetrated more often by excessive drinkers and alcoholics compared to light drinkers. In addition, alcohol use by the offender, victim, or both has been reported in about one third to one half of all incidents of sexual assault.

The relationship between heavy drinking patterns and violence offers an opportunity to address those individuals most at risk for being victims as well as perpetrators of violent acts. This approach seeks to reduce the potential for harm and target patterns of drinking and other behaviors that may increase the chance of a violent act being committed.

Individual Contributing Factors

Several models have been offered to help explain the relationship between alcohol and violence at the individual level. One model suggests that alcohol causes violent behavior through its psychopharmacological effects, such as impairment of cognitive processes that affect perceptions of and attention to cues, interpersonal communication, awareness of consequences, behavioral inhibition, and judgment. According to this line of argumentation, such impairment increases the risks for violence. In addition, chronic intoxication may contribute to subsequent aggression due to factors such as withdrawal, sleep deprivation, nutritional deficits, impairment of neuropsychological functioning, or enhancement of psychopathologic personality disorders. . . .

A second model suggests that violent behavior leads to heavy alcohol use. This model is based on the assumption that violent individuals often choose peer groups and lifestyles that

Alcohol Not the Cause of Domestic Violence

It is commonly assumed that domestic violence is caused by alcohol abuse. This isn't true. The perpetrator is sober in about half of domestic violence cases where the police are called. Also, not all alcoholics or binge drinkers resort to violence when angered or frustrated.

It is how the perpetrator sees himself and his rights that lead to the violence. If a man abuses his family and also tends to have difficulty with controlling his alcohol consumption, he needs to recognise that he has two separate problems.

Better Health Channel,
"Domestic Violence—Why Men Abuse Women,"
August 2006. www.betterhealth.vic.gov.au.

promote heavy drinking. In addition, violent individuals may use alcohol as an excuse to commit a violent act.

A third possible model is the common cause model, which suggests that heavy drinking patterns and violence are related because they share common risk factors rather than a direct causal link. These risk factors include genetic or temperamental traits, antisocial personality disorder, parental modeling of heavy drinking and aggression, and poor relations with parents. Although there is strong support for this model, there are also unique factors that determine whether an individual will become a heavy drinker, a violent offender, or both.

Drinking Context

In addition to individual factors, it has been argued that the drinking context plays a strong role in the association between alcohol and violence. In other words, there are certain settings or situations in which alcohol-related violence is more likely to occur than in others. These settings include bars and sporting events, where fighting or other kinds of violence may take place.

It has been argued that bars and other drinking establishments are crime "hot spots" since they bring together motivated offenders and suitable targets in the absence of effective social control. For example, in the United Kingdom, violence around pubs and clubs occurs most often on weekend nights. Rates of violence have been found to be highest around pub closing times, as crowds of intoxicated strangers converge on the street at the same time. In addition, certain characteristics of licensed establishments—for example, noise, inconvenient access routes, poor ventilation, overcrowding, permissive social environments, and aggressive staff—may make them more conducive to fighting and violence. . . .

Cultural Factors

Internationally, violence is among the leading causes of injury and death for people aged 15 to 44. The rates of alcohol use by both offenders and victims of violent acts vary across studies and across countries. While cross-national comparisons suggest that violence associated with alcohol consumption may be similar in some countries, in others, there is a significant difference. For example, rates are higher in Northern and Eastern Europe than in Southern European countries. This difference has been attributed to views on both alcohol and violence in these countries and to the norms and patterns of drinking within different communities.

As a general rule, cultures in which alcohol use is well-integrated into everyday functions (as in Mediterranean countries) have much lower rates of alcohol-related violence than cultures where alcohol is not well integrated (as in Nordic countries) or cultures that are ambivalent about the role of alcohol in society (as the United States). This difference is likely attributable in part to variations in drinking patterns.

Violence appears to be related to high-quantity consumption. Where excessive drinking or acute intoxication are more common, there is a greater likelihood that it may be associated with violence than in cultures where drinking may be frequent but the quantities are lower. In addition, and equally as important, the relationship of alcohol to violence is strongest in societies that condone violent behavior.

However, it must be noted that alcohol may be involved in violence only among certain individuals and only under some conditions and situations. A model that takes this into account, incorporating elements of the individual and contextual models and cultural variables offered above, is likely to offer a more accurate reflection of the nature of this complex relationship.

Implications for Prevention and Policy

The existing research on the role of alcohol in violence makes it clear that one singular model cannot account for the alcohol-violence relationship in all incidents and for all individuals. Similarly, not all strategies are equally effective in curbing the occurrence of violence involving heavy drinking. Initiatives that attempt to reduce incidents of excessive consumption and targeted interventions that deal with drinking environments may help reduce violence where alcohol is involved.

Intervention strategies that reduce aggressive behavior in general are also needed, particularly within certain populations. Thus, special measures may be developed to target individuals who are at high risk or are already exhibiting aggressive tendencies. While targeted approaches are needed to address the association between certain drinking patterns and violence, policy and prevention initiatives need to integrate a range of factors in order to be effective.

Since alcohol-related violence is most likely to be associated with heavy and problematic drinking patterns, measures that attempt to modify such behaviors may be a useful tool. Increasing awareness among individuals of positive and negative drinking patterns and their possible outcomes is an important first step. Screening for problem drinkers may be appropriate in many instances, followed by counseling for those who are found to be at risk. . . .

Other broader approaches include changing environmental conditions in order to decrease the likelihood of violent incidents in general. Strategies include measures around the management and design of drinking establishments and other venues to reduce factors that may contribute to aggressive behavior and violent outbreaks. . . . Other approaches rely on increasing social control through better enforcement and cooperative measures that involve the community as a whole. It is important to realize that the reduction of violence, including violence associated with some drinking patterns, requires collective involvement of any community and needs to rely on partnerships. Only a concerted effort and a responsibility shared by government, law enforcement, business, educators, parents, clergy, and many others can hope to effect the culture change ultimately required to change violent behavior.

A Complex Issue

In addressing the issue of drinking and violence, it is important to acknowledge that most drinking does not lead to violence and that violent behavior is associated with a number of other aspects. Those violent incidents that involve alcohol generally also involve harmful or abusive drinking patterns.

As a result, targeted interventions around violence and alcohol would benefit from a focus on those drinking patterns that are associated with harm. Developing approaches to modify these patterns helps minimize risks. However, effective interventions are also predicated upon the inclusion of other approaches that target not only the drinking pattern, context, and environment, but also address the root of the problem through education, coping skills, and changing of expectancies and views on inter-gender and interpersonal relationships.

Given the complexity of the issue, it is therefore important to adopt a multifaceted approach to reducing violence associated with drinking, focusing primarily on the violence and on removing the drinking component as a contributing factor. Such approaches can only be successful if they have broad participation and include various segments in society that play a role in shaping perceptions and culture and that ensure the maintenance of social controls.

| "Underage alcohol use remains an intractable health and public safety problem."

Underage Drinking Is a Serious Problem

U.S. Department of Health and Human Services

Underage alcohol use is a widespread and serious problem argues the U.S. Department of Health and Human Services in the following viewpoint. According to the department, it causes numerous public health and safety problems, including motor vehicle crashes, suicide, violence, homicide, assault, and rape. The department recommends policies that delay the beginning of alcohol use as long as possible. The Department of Health and Human Services, a government agency, attempts to protect the health of all Americans.

As you read, consider the following questions:

1. What is the single greatest mortality risk for underage drinkers, according to the author?
2. As cited by the Department of Health and Human Services, what percentage of college rapes involve alcohol use?

U.S. Department of Health and Human Services, *A Comprehensive Plan for Preventing and Reducing Underage Drinking*, January 2006. www.stopalcoholabuse.gov.

3. According to the author what are the social costs of
   underage drinking?

Despite laws against underage drinking in all fifty States
and despite decades of federal, state, and local efforts, as
well as efforts by many private entities, to reduce underage
drinking, alcohol is the most widely consumed substance of
abuse among America's young, used more often than tobacco
or marijuana. Underage alcohol use remains an intractable
health and public safety problem with severe consequences for
youth, their families, and communities. Alcohol accounts for
more deaths than all other illicit drugs combined for adults
and those under age 21. Yet a lack of public recognition of
these consequences and their costs to individuals and society
hampers implementation of a comprehensive prevention effort.

Sources of Underage Drinking Data

The Federal Government funds three major national surveys
to gather information that includes data on underage drinking: the annual "National Survey on Drug Use and Health"
(NSDUH), formerly called the "National Household Survey of
Drug Abuse" (NHSDA), has a representative sample of 12–to
20–year-olds and is sponsored by the Substance Abuse and
Mental Health Services Administration; "Monitoring the Future" (MTF) annually surveys 8th, 10th and 12th graders and
is funded by the National Institute on Drug Abuse (NIDA)
and conducted by the University of Michigan's Institute for
Social Research; and the biannual "Youth Risk Behavior Surveillance System" (YRBSS) surveys 9th through 12th grade
students using a national school-based survey conducted by
CDC as well as state and local school-based surveys conducted
by education and health agencies. Other surveys used by the
government include the National Epidemiologic Survey on Alcohol and Related Conditions (NESARC) conducted by the
National Institute on Alcohol Abuse and Alcoholism (NIAAA)

as well as the Worldwide Surveys of Substance Abuse and Health Behaviors Among Military Personnel conducted by the Department of Defense, both of which contain information on drinkers aged 18 and older. Data from these and other surveys and research efforts provide a disturbing picture of underage alcohol use in America.

Some of the principal findings of governmental surveys and other research related to underage alcohol use are described in the following paragraphs.

Underage Alcohol Use Is Widespread

Underage alcohol use in America is a widespread and serious problem as evidenced by the following data:

- *Current Use*: The 2004 NSDUH reported that approximately 29% of Americans aged 12 through 20 (or about 10.8 million minors) reported having at least one drink in the 30 days prior to the survey. Of this age group, 19.6% (or nearly 7.4 million) were binge drinkers, meaning that they had drunk 5 or more drinks on the same occasion (i.e., at the same time or within a couple of hours of each other) on at least 1 day within the past 30 days. Of those in the 12 to 20 age group, 6.3% (or 2.4 million) were heavy drinkers, meaning that they had drunk 5 or more drinks on the same occasion on each of 5 or more days in the past 30 days. All heavy alcohol users are also binge alcohol users. These figures were essentially unchanged from the 2002 and 2003 surveys.

- *Lifetime Use*: Data from the 2004 MTF survey of U.S. youth show that 75.1% of 12th graders, 63.2% of 10th graders, and 41.0% of 8th graders have drunk alcohol at some point in their lives.

- *Binge Use*: According to data from the 2004 NSDUH, 5.6% of 14-year-olds, 18.3% of 16-year-olds, 33.1% of 18-year-olds, and 40.3% of 20-year-olds had engaged in binge drinking within the past 30 days.

- *Heavy Use*: Data from the 2004 NSDUH survey show that 4.5% of 16-year-olds, 11.0% of 18-year-olds, and 16.3% of 20-year-olds had engaged in heavy alcohol consumption within the past 30 days.

- *Use to Intoxication*: According to 2005 data from the 2004 MTF survey, 57.5% of 12th graders, 42.1% of 10th graders, and 19.5% of 8th graders reported having been drunk at least once in their lives.

- *Use to Intoxication Within the Last Month*: Data from the MTF survey for 2005 indicates that 30.2% of 12th graders, 17.6% of 10th graders, and 6.0% of 8th graders reported having been drunk in the past month.

Youth Start Drinking at an Early Age

Studies show that drinking often begins at very young ages. Data from recent surveys indicate that approximately:

- Ten percent of 9–10 year olds have already started drinking

- Nearly one-third of underage drinkers begin before age 13

- The peak years of initiation are 7th through 11th grades, based on data from high school seniors

Youths who report drinking prior to the age of 15 are more likely to develop substance abuse problems, to engage in risky sexual behavior, and to experience other negative consequences in comparison to those who begin at a later time. The age of onset of drinking, therefore, is a marker for future problems, including heavier use of alcohol and other drugs during adolescence and the development of an alcohol dependence diagnosis in adulthood. Delaying the age of onset of first alcohol use as long as possible can ameliorate some of the negative consequences associated with underage alcohol consumption. Therefore, whether underage drinkers are starting at younger or older ages over a given period of years is a matter of concern. . . .

Underage drinking is both an individual and societal problem, a matter of public safety and of public health with profound consequences for the young, their families, and their communities. It is a complex problem that has plagued society for generations and results in a range of adverse short- and long-term consequences. Some of these adverse consequences are described in the following paragraphs. In addition to the negatives effects of underage drinking on the drinker, a number of consequences also result to those around him or her, which are referred to as secondary effects.

Motor Vehicle Crashes and Other Alcohol-Related Accidents

The greatest single mortality risk for underage drinkers is motor vehicle crashes. In 2002, 6,788 persons aged 15 to 20 were involved in fatal crashes and 29% of the drivers in this age group who were killed had been drinking. Relative to adults, young people who drink and drive have an increased risk of alcohol-related crashes because of their relative inexperience behind the wheel and their increased impairment from alcohol. According to survey data, about 5.9% of 16-year-olds, 12.6% of 17-year-olds, 16.4% of 18-year-olds, 21.1% of 19-year-olds, and 23.4% of 20-year-olds reported driving under the influence of alcohol in 2003. The reported prevalence of driving under the influence of alcohol increases with age until 25, after which it declines. Over all, 30.2% of high school stu-

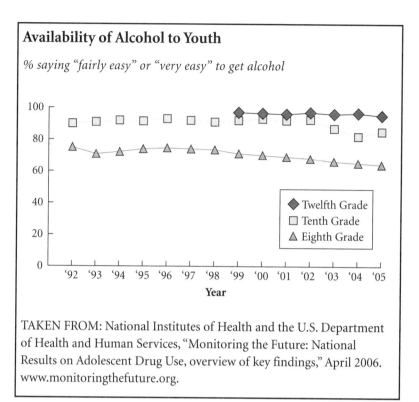

Availability of Alcohol to Youth

% saying "fairly easy" or "very easy" to get alcohol

Legend:
◆ Twelfth Grade
□ Tenth Grade
△ Eighth Grade

TAKEN FROM: National Institutes of Health and the U.S. Department of Health and Human Services, "Monitoring the Future: National Results on Adolescent Drug Use, overview of key findings," April 2006. www.monitoringthefuture.org.

dents reported that, within the past 30 days, they had ridden with a driver who had been drinking. For seniors, that figure rose to 33.3%.

In 2002, 2,569 individuals ages 16 to 20 died from unintentional injuries other than motor vehicle crashes, such as poisonings, drownings, falls, burns, etc. Research suggests that approximately 40% of these deaths were alcohol-related.

Violence, Suicide, and Alcohol

In 2002, 2,732 young people ages 12 to 20 died from homicide and 2,196 from suicide. At present, we do not know exactly how many of these deaths are alcohol related. One study estimated that for all ages combined nearly half of the homicides and almost a third of the suicides were alcohol-related. Another study of deaths among those under 21 reported that over a third of the homicides were alcohol-related as were 12% of male suicides and 8% of female suicides.

Individuals under the age of 21 commit 45% of rapes, 44% of robberies, and 37% of other assaults. It is estimated that for the population as a whole, 50% of violent crime is related to alcohol use. The degree to which violent crime committed by those under 21 is alcohol-related remains to be determined.

It is estimated that 90% of college rapes involve the use of alcohol by the assailant, the victim, or both. About 97,000 college students are victims of sexual assault or date rape related to alcohol use each year. Alcohol use is involved in 95% of all violent crime on college campuses.

More than 600,000 college students are assaulted by another student who has been drinking, and another 500,000 students were unintentionally injured while under the influence of alcohol.

Other Risky Behaviors

A variety of other risky behaviors are associated with underage alcohol use. Some of these behaviors include riding with a driver who has been drinking, unplanned and unprotected sexual activity, and carrying a weapon to school. Although the data indicate that alcohol use is correlated with these risky behaviors, the data cannot prove causation between alcohol use and the behavior. Nevertheless, it is known that alcohol can impair an individual's decision-making capacity and that it reduces inhibitions. Therefore, drinking may be related to the decision to engage in risky behavior, particularly in adolescents whose judgment and decision-making capabilities are still developing.

Potential Brain Impairment

Brain impairment is one of the potential long-term risks of underage alcohol consumption. Neurobiological research suggests that adolescence may be a period of unique vulnerability to the effects of alcohol. For example, early heavy alcohol use may have negative effects on the actual physical development of the brain structure of adolescents as well as on brain functioning. Negative effects indicated by neurological studies include decreased ability in planning, executive functioning, memory, spatial operations, and attention, all of which play an important role in academic performance and future levels of functioning.

Increased Risk of Developing an Alcohol Use Disorder

The early onset of alcohol use (at age 14 or younger) in combination with an escalation of drinking in adolescence have both been documented in a number of studies as risk factors for the development of alcohol-related problems in adulthood. The onset of alcohol consumption in childhood or early adolescence is a marker for later alcohol-related problems, including heavier adolescent use of alcohol and other drugs and the development of alcohol abuse or dependence in adulthood. Persons aged 21 or older who reported first use of alcohol before age 14 were more than 6 times as likely to report past year alcohol dependence or abuse than persons who first used alcohol at age 21 or older.

Other Negative Consequences of Underage Drinking

Other consequences of underage drinking include death from alcohol poisoning, academic problems, various social problems, and physical problems such as medical illnesses.

The social costs of underage drinking are conservatively estimated at $53 billion, including $19 billion from traffic crashes and $29 billion from violent crime.

The social, individual, and economic consequences of underage drinking make it a leading health problem in the United States, one that has remained stubbornly resistant to a variety of measures initiated to prevent and reduce it over the past three decades. Because adult alcohol use is an accepted part of American life, underage drinking must be addressed within that context. The primary preventive issue in underage drinking is to delay onset of alcohol use as long as possible—preferably until the age of 21. Yet that delay must be achieved within an environment in which alcohol is readily available to most underage youth and is attractive to them. A comprehensive plan involving federal, state, and local governments; organizations and institutions in the private sector; concerned individuals; and the parents of underage youth is critical if progress is to be made against this intractable health problem.

> *"Many successful Americans have a history of high school and college alcohol use—sometimes involving periods of excess."*

The Risks of Underage Drinking Have Been Exaggerated

Maia Szalavitz

While underage drinking can have serious consequences, these consequences are often exaggerated, maintains Maia Szalavitz in the following viewpoint. She argues that many youth drink without serious problems and that demonizing alcohol and instituting zero tolerance approaches for youth can actually be harmful. She points out that cultures that teach youth how to drink responsibly, rather than banning drinking altogether, tend to have fewer alcohol-related problems among youth. Szalavitz is a senior fellow for the Statistical Assessment Service, a nonprofit organization that works to correct scientific misinformation in the media.

Maia Szalavitz, "Underage Drinking," *Statistical Assessment Service*, April 29, 2005, pp. 1–3. http://alcoholnews.org. Reproduced by permission.

As you read, consider the following questions:

1. According to a PIRE study, as cited by Szalavitz, what percentage of car accident deaths caused by drivers twenty-one and under are related to intoxication?

2. As explained by the author, how can a college student at a party be defined as a binge drinker without ever reaching intoxication?

3. According to Szalavitz, what do most experts agree on regarding zero tolerance policies?

Can you honestly say that you never drank alcohol during high school? If so, you are in a distinct minority: nearly 80% of high school seniors admit to at least trying a drink and about 50 percent report having consumed alcohol during the last month. While these numbers are down from their peaks in the late 70s and early 80s, a large majority of young people still drink regularly long before they reach the legal age of 21.

Clearly, efforts to eliminate underage drinking have failed. It is also plain that many successful Americans have a history of high school and college alcohol use—sometimes involving periods of excess. If youthful drinking were a genuine bar to political office, higher education or career advancement, government, academia and industry would grind to a halt.

Exaggerating the Risk

Nonetheless, the media and some activist groups, government agencies and foundations constantly promote the idea that most teen drinking is extremely risky and carries a high probability of causing alcoholism or death. For example, an August 2004 press release from the Office of Juvenile Justice and Delinquency Prevention and the National Liquor Law Enforcement Association screams, "The carnage caused by underage drinking in America is unrelenting," and notes that alcohol kills "6.5 more kids than all other drugs combined."

Similarly, a recent CNN [Cable News Network] medical segment ["Teenage binge drinkers are more likely to become adult alcoholics" June 16, 2004] reported that a study had found that teen binge drinking was linked to an increased risk for alcoholism. CNN mentioned that 70% of teens binge drink—but did not note that only 3.81% of adults are alcoholics. The channel's physician-reporter Sanjay Gupta ended his report with a conclusion not backed by the data he cited, saying, "So really, the message to parents out of this is even a small drink, even only a sip early on in life could be a problem later on."

Headlines like the *San Francisco Chronicle*'s "Teenage Drinking a U.S. Epidemic" [February 26, 2002] and the *New York Post*'s "Boozed-Up Teens in Dangerous Liaisons," [February 7, 2002] shout along with the advocates' PR [public relations] campaigns, often including hyped-up quotes from people like the National Center on Addiction and Substance Abuse (CASA)'s head Joe Califano, such as "Alcohol is the fatal attraction for many teens."

As a result, politicians call for ever stricter legislation; activists say that alcohol advertising is targeting teens and should be banned; and schools enact "zero tolerance" policies that expel kids for doing once what the vast majority of American adults did many times at their age.

Do these efforts make sense? Are we using our resources wisely by trying to prevent all teens from taking a sip till 21—or could we better spend our money by focusing on reducing the genuine harm that can occur when some young people drink to excess?

Alcohol-Related Deaths Lower than Expected

According to a 1999 study conducted by the Pacific Institute on Research and Evaluation (PIRE), about 3,500 deaths per year are caused by drinkers under the age of 21. Homicides account for the greatest number of these deaths (roughly 1,600 per year), followed by drunk driving (1,400), and teen suicides (260). The remaining 300-odd deaths are caused by other accidents, drownings, burns, and alcohol overdoses.

Interestingly, the proportion of deaths judged to be alcohol-related was lower than one might expect from the hysterical coverage teen drinking is usually given in the media. For example, just under 20% of car accident deaths caused by drivers 21 and younger are related to intoxication—and this proportion has been dropping for the last 20 years.

The PIRE researchers also estimated that 21% of murders committed by youth were caused by alcohol. This was based on research showing that 42% of killers report being intoxicated at the time of their crime and on other studies which found that while half of alcohol-linked killings would probably have occurred even if alcohol hadn't been consumed by the perpetrator, the other half would not have taken place if the killer had been sober. The figures for suicide were even lower, with just 12% of male suicides and eight percent of those committed by females attributable to alcohol.

But while the PIRE analysis looked at deaths caused by intoxicated youth, it didn't separate out which of those deaths occurred among other young people. Another analysis tried to calculate this number, seeking to determine the number of deaths of youth aged 10–19 related to alcohol.

Using 1995 figures, it found a very similar number to that compiled by PIRE: 3,300 deaths of young people could be attributed to alcohol-related incidents, including homicides, suicides, car accidents and alcohol overdoses.

From this report and the census population estimate of teens aged 10–19 in 1995, a very rough estimate of the risk of alcohol-related death in this age group can be calculated. The odds of a teen dying an alcohol-related death come to approximately .00009 per year or 9 in 100,000. If one calculates the figure only among those who admit to drinking in the last month, the figure is still less than 2/100ths of one percent.

Costs of Deaths and Injuries

This still represents a significant proportion of the untimely deaths among youth: the total number of deaths among those aged 10–19 in 1995 was 14,600, meaning that 23% of adolescent deaths that year can be blamed on alcohol. And while the risk of death is relatively low, the risk of injury is not. The PIRE study estimated that about 1 million non-fatal injuries were caused by underage drunk drivers and 1 million assaults were committed by youth under the influence of alcohol. About 5,100 injuries were related to drunken suicide attempts and 40,000 to the results of alcohol poisoning. These estimates relied on statistics from the CDC's [Centers for Disease Control] National Hospital Ambulatory Medical Care Survey.

The PIRE study estimated the costs related to underage drinking at $52.8 billion per year. The vast majority of these costs—$38.5 billion—were related to loss of quality of life due to deaths and serious injuries from car accidents and violent assaults. These figures are calculated by determining what people are willing to pay to reduce their risk of incurring such harms—they do not derive from pay-outs in lawsuits or actual government expenditures. Actual lost income and other non-health related costs related to youth drinking added up to $10.6 billion, while medical costs amounted to $3.6 billion. . . .

Misleading Research

Throughout the 1990s and the early 2000s, fears about alcohol and teens were continually stoked by the media and by organizations with a stake in pushing the notion that drinking is a great danger to youth.

For example, there was the study—"Teen Tipplers: America's Underage Drinking Epidemic"—released by the Center on Addiction and Substance Abuse (CASA) in 2002 claiming that people under 21 drunk 25% of all the alcohol consumed in the United States. This prompted dozens of headlines in newspapers across the country about a teen alcohol "epidemic" that year. (Unfortunately, CASA failed to take into account that the government deliberately over-sampled teens, and as a result its analysis misrepresented their proportion in the population.)

There were also numerous reports claiming that young people were increasingly engaged in binge drinking, many stemming from research by Henry Weschler at the Harvard School of Public Health. For example, the *Washington Post* headlined one article, citing the researcher, "Drinking Lessons; As Alcohol Problems Grow, Colleges Seek New Remedies" [April 4, 2002]. But these accounts rely on such a liberal definition of binging (which Wechsler himself promotes) that it includes those with blood alcohol levels (BACs) well below the legal limits for driving.

Rather than seeing a binge as being a spree of drinking lasting a day or more, as many people would colloquially define it, alcohol researchers have now classified a binge as being a situation in which someone takes "5 or more drinks on one occasion." This means that a college student who has a drink an hour during a long party—and never reaches intoxication—is a "binge drinker." Not surprisingly, this has led to a majority of high school seniors and college kids being defined as bingers.

Zero Tolerance Policies

Given such studies and the increasing calls for action by activists and concerned parents, educators and policy makers decided that something had to be done. It was already illegal for teens to drink, so high schools began setting "zero tolerance" policies. These took off in the wake of the Columbine High School shootings, and targeted alcohol and drugs along with weapons, even though none of the school shootings was linked to alcohol or recreational drugs.

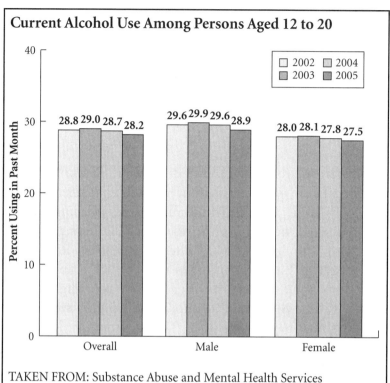

Current Alcohol Use Among Persons Aged 12 to 20

Percent Using in Past Month

2002   2004
2003   2005

Overall: 28.8 29.0 28.7 28.2

Male: 29.6 29.9 29.6 28.9

Female: 28.0 28.1 27.8 27.5

TAKEN FROM: Substance Abuse and Mental Health Services Administration, "Results from the 2005 National Survey on Drug Use and Health: National Findings," September 2006. www.oas.samhsa.gov.

These policies meant that if a high schooler was caught—sometimes even off-campus—with one drink on one occasion, he or she would be permanently expelled. For example, in 1998, four teens from a Colorado school who had never been in trouble before, were expelled from their high school for having admitted to drinking in a motel room on one occasion. [*Monument County Tribune*, October 1, 1998]. In another case, a California teen became suicidal after being expelled for drinking off-campus one day during his lunch hour. He never completed high school. In some cases, the mandatory punishment is less severe: the teen is sent to treatment instead.

Problems with Zero Tolerance

While the legal drinking age is a matter of debate amongst alcohol policy experts, even the most conservative alcohol policy groups like CASA do not support extreme zero tolerance, recognizing that expulsion from school does more damage to a kid's future than most drinking incidents do. Not only does expulsion give kids more time to drink (and a reason to drown their sorrows), research suggests that higher education itself reduces the odds of long-term alcoholism.

Even mandated treatment poses problems if it is used indiscriminately. While teens with genuine drinking problems may benefit, those who were just unlucky enough to get caught experimenting can be harmed by being grouped with kids with more severe problems. Forcing kids to admit that they are alcoholics in order to successfully complete treatment—as most teen treatment programs do—may also be dangerous. Telling teens, who are often confused about their identities to begin with, that they have the lifelong disease of alcoholism (which they are told, carries a 90% chance of relapse) can be a self-fulfilling prophecy.

Almost all experts now agree—from CASA to the ABA [American Beverage Association] to the ACLU [American Civil Liberties Union]—that zero tolerance policies have more risks than benefits (though CASA supports tough policies if kids are given treatment, not expulsion). Drinking during the school day is certainly unacceptable; but not all underage drinkers are drinking for the same reasons: One kid may be an alcoholic, while another may have parents going through a nasty divorce, and yet another is a shy straight-A student trying to be more sociable. A school's response should take these circumstances into account and not sacrifice one child's future in hopes of deterring others.

There's just no evidence that supports a deterrent effect for these policies and a great deal which suggests that they can do harm. For example, researchers at Harvard's Civil Rights project found that high rates of suspension from school (which are linked with zero tolerance because it mandates such punishment for first offenses) are linked with high rates of juvenile incarceration. Previous studies found no evidence that zero tolerance policies improved school performance or atmosphere.

Policy Alternatives

So what does the research support in terms of policies and programs that reduce youth drinking and the harms related to it?

Some experts like Stanton Peele, author of the classic text, *The Meaning of Addiction*, point to wine-drinking cultures like those in Italy, France and Spain for hints on how to handle alcohol policy better. In these cultures, alcohol is essentially a food—it is part of a meal and children learn to drink with their parents from a very early age. Drunkenness is not tolerated. Though rates of daily drinking are high in these cultures, rates of binging and other alcohol problems have, historically, been low. Alcohol itself is viewed as a neutral substance; it is drunkenness and not drinking that is seen as the problem.

In contrast, northern drinking cultures see alcohol as almost a mystical substance—with great power for good or ill. Drinking is an activity in and of itself; alcohol is consumed in bars not at family meals, and it is often positively associated with masculinity. In such settings, drunkenness is frequently the goal of drinking. Northern drinking cultures typically have lower rates of daily drinking but higher rates of binging, alcohol-related problems and complete abstinence. The U.S. has generally followed the northern pattern.

Lately, however, drinking-to-get-drunk behavior has become popular in southern Europe (possibly as a result of the large influx of young drink-oriented tourists from northern countries), proving that these cultures are not totally immune from alcohol-related problems.

Nevertheless, the southern, demystified view of alcohol as part of a meal may be worth adopting. Viewing alcohol as a "demon" allows those who drink to excess to avoid responsibility for their behavior and place the blame on the substance. By contrast, seeing it as something most people manage responsibly re-enforces self-control.

Periodical Bibliography

The following articles have been selected to supplement the diverse views presented in this chapter.

David Gargill and Howie Kahn	"Drink: Raise Your Spirits," *GQ*, December 2006.
Christine Gorman	"What Alcohol Does to a Child," *Time*, June 5, 2006.
Diana Kohnle	"Alcohol: A Bigger Threat to U.S. Youth than Drugs," *HealthDay*, June 29, 2006.
Alexis Kwiatkowski	"Drinking Alcohol Just Adds Problems," *Post-Standard*, March 20, 2007.
Ted R. Miller, David T. Levy, Rebecca S. Spicer, et al.	"Societal Costs of Underage Drinking," *Journal of Studies on Alcohol*, July 2006.
Clayton Neighbors, Casey J. Spieker, Laura Oster-Aaland, et al.	"Celebration Intoxication," *Journal of American College Health*, September 2005.
Heather Ogilvie	"A Different Approach to Treating Alcoholism," *Consumers' Research Magazine*, June 2002.
Richard Rice	"College Drinking: Norms vs. Perceptions," *Scientist*, February 2006.
Susan Schindehette	"Dying for a Drink," *People Weekly*, September 4, 2006.
Shane Watson	"Drink: Self-Medicating with Alcohol Is a Natural Response to the Human Condition," *New Statesman*, May 8, 2006.
Columbus Ledger-Enquirer	"Where They Drink, When They Drink, and How They Conceal It—Teens Talk to Us About Their World of Alcohol," October 24, 2006.

CHAPTER 3

What Are the Causes of Alcohol Abuse?

Chapter Preface

Alcohol abuse is a serious problem for many people. According to the Centers for Disease Control, it can result in myriad problems for the drinker and society. The agency states: "Alcohol abuse . . . results in harm to one's health, interpersonal relationships and ability to work. . . . [It can also cause] failure to fulfill responsibilities at work, school or home; drinking in dangerous situations such as while driving; legal problems associated with alcohol use and continued drinking despite problems that are caused or worsened by drinking."

In the United States, alcohol abuse is very common, often goes untreated, and costs the country billions of dollars every year. The Substance Abuse and Mental Health Services Administration estimates that 7.6 percent of Americans age twelve or older meet the criteria for alcohol dependence or abuse. According to a 2006 report by the National Center on Addiction and Substance Abuse at Columbia University (CASA), underage drinkers are much more likely than adults to suffer from alcohol abuse or dependence. The center found that 25.9 percent of underage drinkers met the clinical criteria for alcohol abuse or dependence, compared to 9.6 percent of adult drinkers. Research shows that most people with alcohol abuse problems do not receive treatment. For example, in a 2006 series of articles, media company Public Access Journalism reports that nine out of ten Americans who are addicted to alcohol or other drugs do not receive treatment. Reasons for this lack of treatment include misunderstanding of alcohol abuse, denial, shame, and the inability to pay for treatment.

The costs of untreated alcohol abuse in the United States are high. According to Joseph A. Califano Jr., president of CASA, alcohol abuse and dependence cost the country approximately $220 billion in 2005, more than either cancer or obesity. This cost includes lost productivity, health care costs, criminal justice system costs, social welfare administration, and property losses from alcohol-related motor vehicle crashes and fires.

In an effort to reduce the many costs of alcohol abuse, and to help the high percentage of people suffering from it, researchers are attempting to understand what causes it. As the following chapters reveal, however, there are differing opinions on this issue.

> *"The craving that an alcoholic feels for alcohol can be as strong as the need for food and water. An alcoholic will continue to drink despite serious family, health, or legal problems."*

Alcoholism Is a Disease

National Institute on Alcohol Abuse and Alcoholism

In the following viewpoint, the U.S. National Institute on Alcohol Abuse and Alcoholism (NIAAA) explains that alcoholism is a disease that, like diabetes or high blood pressure, can be inherited. While it can be treated with counseling and various medications, alcoholism cannot be cured, maintains NIAAA, and it lasts a person's whole lifetime. In the organization's opinion, the best treatment for alcoholism is to stop drinking completely. NIAAA is the leading U.S. agency for research on alcohol abuse, alcoholism, and other health effects of alcohol.

As you read, consider the following questions:

1. In addition to a person's genes, what other factor influences the development of alcoholism, according to NIAAA?

2. According to the author, how does naltrexone treat alcoholism?

National Institute on Alcohol Abuse and Alcoholism, *FAQs for the General Public*, January 2007. www.niaaa.nih.gov.

3. As stated by NIAAA, how many people in the United States abuse alcohol or are alcohol dependent?

Alcoholism, also known as alcohol dependence, is a disease that includes the following four symptoms:

- *Craving*—A strong need, or urge, to drink.

- *Loss of control*—Not being able to stop drinking once drinking has begun.

- *Physical dependence*—Withdrawal symptoms, such as nausea, sweating, shakiness, and anxiety after stopping drinking.

- *Tolerance*—The need to drink greater amounts of alcohol to get "high."

For clinical and research purposes, formal diagnostic criteria for alcoholism also have been developed. Such criteria are included in the *Diagnostic and Statistical Manual of Mental Disorders, Fourth Edition*, published by the American Psychiatric Association, as well as in the *International Classification of Diseases*, published by the World Health Organization. . . .

What Causes Alcoholism

Is alcoholism a disease?

Yes, alcoholism is a disease. The craving that an alcoholic feels for alcohol can be as strong as the need for food or water. An alcoholic will continue to drink despite serious family, health, or legal problems.

Like many other diseases, alcoholism is chronic, meaning that it lasts a person's lifetime; it usually follows a predictable course; and it has symptoms. The risk for developing alcoholism is influenced both by a person's genes and by his or her lifestyle. . . .

Alcohol and Genetics

What's also increasingly clear is that many genes play a role and that genes work both ways—with some protecting people against alcoholism and others greatly raising the risk. . .said Dr. Mary-Anne Enoch, a research physician at the National Institute of Alcohol Abuse and Alcoholism.

Certain groups of people, for instance, like many Japanese, Chinese and Jews, carry genes that *protect* against alcoholism by raising levels of particular liver enzymes so that it's unpleasant to keep drinking because of nausea, flushing and rapid heart beat.

Others, including many Caucasians, carry genes that act in the brain rather than the liver and *raise* the risk of becoming an alcoholic, although if people with these genes never touch a drop, they will never become alcoholics. Overall, those with a parent or sibling who is alcoholic, are at three to four times the normal risk.

Judy Foreman, *"Alcoholism: A Disease or a Moral Failing,"* My Health Sense, *October 19, 2004. www.myhealthsense.com.*

Is alcoholism inherited?

Research shows that the risk for developing alcoholism does indeed run in families. The genes a person inherits partially explain this pattern, but lifestyle is also a factor. Currently, researchers are working to discover the actual genes that put people at risk for alcoholism. Your friends, the amount of stress in your life, and how readily available alcohol is also are factors that may increase your risk for alcoholism.

But remember: Risk is not destiny. Just because alcoholism tends to run in families doesn't mean that a child of an alcoholic parent will automatically become an alcoholic too. Some people develop alcoholism even though no one in their family has a drinking problem. By the same token, not all children of alcoholic families get into trouble with alcohol. Knowing you are at risk is important, though, because then you can take steps to protect yourself from developing problems with alcohol. . . .

Treating Alcoholism

Can alcoholism be cured?

No, alcoholism cannot be cured at this time. Even if an alcoholic hasn't been drinking for a long time, he or she can still suffer a relapse. Not drinking is the safest course for most people with alcoholism. . . .

Can alcoholism be treated?

Yes, alcoholism can be treated. Alcoholism treatment programs use both counseling and medications to help a person stop drinking. Treatment has helped many people stop drinking and rebuild their lives. . . .

Which medications treat alcoholism?

Three oral medications—disulfiram (Antabuse®), naltrexone (Depade®, ReVia®), and acamprosate (Campral®)—are currently [as of 2007] approved to treat alcohol dependence. In addition, an injectable, long-acting form of naltrexone (Vivitrol®) is available. These medications have been shown to help people with dependence reduce their drinking, avoid relapse to heavy drinking, and achieve and maintain abstinence. Naltrexone acts in the brain to reduce craving for alcohol after someone has stopped drinking. Acamprosate is thought to work by reducing symptoms that follow lengthy abstinence, such as anxiety and insomnia. Disulfiram discourages drinking by making the person taking it feel sick after drinking alcohol.

Other types of drugs are available to help manage symptoms of withdrawal (such as shakiness, nausea, and sweating) if they occur after someone with alcohol dependence stops drinking.

Although medications are available to help treat alcoholism, there is no "magic bullet." In other words, no single medication is available that works in every case and/or in every person. Developing new and more effective medications to treat alcoholism remains a high priority for researchers. . . .

Does alcoholism treatment work?

Alcoholism treatment works for many people. But like other chronic illnesses, such as diabetes, high blood pressure, and asthma, there are varying levels of success when it comes to treatment. Some people stop drinking and remain sober. Others have long periods of sobriety with bouts of relapse. And still others cannot stop drinking for any length of time. With treatment, one thing is clear, however: the longer a person abstains from alcohol, the more likely he or she will be able to stay sober.

Alcohol Abuse

Do you have to be an alcoholic to experience problems?

No. Alcoholism is only one type of an alcohol problem. Alcohol abuse can be just as harmful. A person can abuse alcohol without actually being an alcoholic—that is, he or she may drink too much and too often but still not be dependent on alcohol. Some of the problems linked to alcohol abuse include not being able to meet work, school, or family responsibilities; drunk-driving arrests and car crashes; and drinking-related medical conditions. Under some circumstances, even social or moderate drinking is dangerous—for example, when driving, during pregnancy, or when taking certain medications. . . .

Prevalence of Alcohol-Related Problems

Are specific groups of people more likely to have problems?

Alcohol abuse and alcoholism cut across gender, race, and nationality. In the United States, 17.6 million people—about 1 in every 12 adults—abuse alcohol or are alcohol dependent.

In general, more men than women are alcohol dependent or have alcohol problems. And alcohol problems are highest among young adults ages 18–29 and lowest among adults ages 65 and older. We also know that people who start drinking at an early age—for example, at age 14 or younger—are at much higher risk of developing alcohol problems at some point in their lives compared to someone who starts drinking at age 21 or after. . . .

How can you tell if someone has a problem?

Answering the following four questions can help you find out if you or a loved one has a drinking problem:

- Have you ever felt you should cut down on your drinking?

- Have people annoyed you by criticizing your drinking?

- Have you ever felt bad or guilty about your drinking?

- Have you ever had a drink first thing in the morning to steady your nerves or to get rid of a hangover?

One "yes" answer suggests a possible alcohol problem. More than one "yes" answer means it is highly likely that a problem exists. If you think that you or someone you know might have an alcohol problem, it is important to see a doctor or other health care provider right away. They can help you determine if a drinking problem exists and plan the best course of action.

Help for Alcohol Problems

Can a problem drinker simply cut down?

It depends. If that person has been diagnosed as an alcoholic, the answer is "no." Alcoholics who try to cut down on drinking rarely succeed. Cutting out alcohol—that is, abstaining—is usually the best course for recovery. People who are not alcohol dependent but who have experienced alcohol-related problems may be able to limit the amount they drink. If they can't stay within those limits, they need to stop drinking altogether. . . .

How can a person get help for an alcohol problem?

There are many national and local resources that can help. The National Drug and Alcohol Treatment Referral Routing Service provides a toll-free telephone number, 1–800–662–HELP (4357), offering various resource information. Through this service you can speak directly to a representative concerning substance abuse treatment, request printed material on alcohol or other drugs, or obtain local substance abuse treatment referral information in your State.

| "Research has shown that alcoholism is a choice, not a disease."

Alcoholism Is Not a Disease

Baldwin Research Institute

According to the Baldwin Research Institute in the following viewpoint, the disease concept of alcoholism is based on fraudulent research and has no scientific basis. This theory has been spread by an alcoholism treatment industry that earns billions of dollars from treatment programs, insists the institute; however, it actually creates a reduced chance of sobriety for alcoholics. In reality, says the institute, alcoholism is a choice, and the best way for alcoholics to recover is to take responsibility for their alcoholism. The Baldwin Research Institute is a nonprofit organization that conducts research and develops programs to facilitate recovery from problems associated with alcohol and other drugs.

As you read, consider the following questions:

1. According to Baldwin Research Institute interviews of 545 substance abusers, how many believed they had a disease, as reported by the author?

2. As reported by the Baldwin Research Institute, what percentage of people in a recent Gallup poll believe that alcoholism is a disease?

3. As argued by the author, what are the success rates of programs that teach choice rather than the disease concept of alcoholism?

History and science have shown us that the existence of the disease of alcoholism is pure speculation. Just saying alcoholism is a disease, doesn't make it true. Nevertheless, medical professionals and American culture lovingly embraced the disease concept and quickly applied it to every possible deviant behavior from alcohol abuse to compulsive lecturing. The disease concept was a panacea for many failing medical institutions adding billions of dollars to the industry and leading to a prompt evolution of pop-psychology. Research has shown that alcoholism is a choice, not a disease, and stripping alcohol abusers of their choice, by applying the disease concept, is a threat to the health of the individual.

The disease concept oozes into every crevice of our society perpetuating harmful misinformation that hurts the very people it was intended to help. It is a backwards situation where the assumptions of a few were adopted as fact by the medical profession, devoid of supporting evidence. And soon after, the disease concept was accepted by the general public. With this said, visiting the history of the disease concept gives us all a better understanding of how and why all of this happened.

Origin of the Disease Concept

The disease concept originated in the 1800s with a fellow by the name of Dr. Benjamin Rush. He believed alcoholics were diseased and used the idea to promote his prohibitionist political platform. He also believed that dishonesty, political dissention and being of African-American decent were diseases. The "disease concept" was used throughout the late 1800s and early 1900s by prohibitionists and those involved in the Temperance Movement to further a political agenda. Prior to this time, the term alcoholic did not exist. Alcohol was freely consumed, but drunkenness was not tolerated. . . . During this period of time social ties and family played a much more influential role in an individual's life. Therefore, deviant behaviors were undesirable and less likely to occur. It was not until industrialization began, when the importance of social and family ties diminished, that alcoholism became a problem. We now live in a society that encourages binge drinking as a social norm, but at the same time, we live in a society that discourages it.

Fraudulent Research

The "recovery" community's adoption of the disease concept began with an early AA [Alcoholics Anonymous] member named Marty Mann. Her efforts, combined with a somewhat dubious scientist named E.M. Jellinek, began national acceptance of the disease concept. It was Jellinek's "scientific" study that opened the door for the medical community's support. E.M. Jellinek's study was funded by the efforts of Marty Mann and R. Brinkley Smithers. And, like so many other circumstances involving Jellinek and Marty Mann, the study was bogus if not outright fraudulent. The surveys he based his conclusions on were from a *hand picked* group of alcoholics. There were 158 questionnaires handed out and 60 of them were suspiciously not included. His conclusion was based on less than 100 hand picked alcoholics chosen by Marty Mann. Ms. Mann, of course, had a personal agenda to remove the stigma about the homeless and dirty alcoholic or "bowery drunk" in order to gain financial support from the wealthy. By removing the stigma, the problem becomes one of the general population, which would then include the wealthy. The first step was Jellinek publishing his findings in his book *The Stages of Alcoholism* which was based on the selective study. Later, E.M. Jellinek was asked by Yale University to refute his own findings. *He complied.* E.M. Jellinek's *Stages of Alcoholism* did not stand up to scientific scrutiny. . . .

It was Jellinek's study that was such a monumental turning point for the supporters of the disease concept. The current disease paradigm was, in part, developed and promulgated by Jellinek and various other partial participants with personal agendas. Today, Jellinek's *Stages of the Alcoholic* is still widely used to diagnose substance abusers. But these stages are based on a corrupt study that the author, himself, later refuted. Jellinek not only published a fraudulent study, he defrauded members of his academic community, and apparently lied about his educational background to gain acceptance. Nonetheless, it was Jellinek's *Stages of the Alcoholic* that led to diagnosing alcoholism as a disease and eventually to the medical acceptance of alcoholism as a disease. Astoundingly, the inception of the current disease and treatment paradigm is based on fraud.

A Damaging Concept for Alcoholics

While many advocate for its benefits, the disease concept has proven to be far more damaging to the substance abuser than anyone could have predicted. Therapists claim the disease concept helps the patient to understand the seriousness of [his/her] problems. But in reality, this idea has backfired. The disease concept strips the substance abuser of responsibility. A disease cannot be cured by force of will; therefore, adding the medical label transfers the responsibility from the abuser to caregivers. Inevitably the abusers become unwilling victims, and just as inevitably they take on that role. In retrospect then, the disease concept has effectively increased alcoholism and drug abuse. Furthermore, its only benefit has been vast monetary reward for the professionals' and governmental agencies responsible for providing recovery services. Specifically, it has not offered a solution for those attempting to stop abusive alcohol and drug use.

The Danger of Giving Up Responsibility

The danger of constantly telling people that they have no control is that eventually they may come to believe it. Falling off the wagon thus only proves to the drinker what he has been told: that he has no control. Henceforth, what is his motivation to keep attending AA [Alcoholics Anonymous] or to seek further treatment? Treatment professionals who advocate "12 Step" programs typically regard relapse not as a failure of treatment, but as a failure of the patient to comply with treatment. Given these conditions, it is no wonder so few people are able to maintain long-term sobriety through "12 Step" recovery programs.

On the other hand, when you tell someone that, with time and effort, he can change his habits, make improvements to troublesome aspects of his life, and reverse the course of his drinking problems, he will probably be more willing to give treatment a try and recognize the signs of his progress. By showing him he has choices for treatment, you provide more hope and give him back a sense of control simply by allowing him to choose.

Heather Ogilvie, "A Different Approach to Treating Alcoholism,"
Consumers' Research Magazine, *June 2002.*

Baldwin Research Institute, Inc. interviewed 545 self-acknowledged substance abusers. Out of the 545, 454 of them had been to at least one conventional, disease-based treatment facility prior to the interview. Some had been to as many as 20 or more conventional, disease-based treatment facilities prior to the interview. Of the total 545 substance abusers, 542 never thought they had a disease. Rather, they thought they had made poor choices regarding their substance use. Three thought they had a disease, and it should be noted that those three were continuing to abuse substances. For those who did not think they had a disease, more than 400 of them falsely stated during conventional treatment that they believed they had a disease. The pressure to conform to the treatment rhetoric and the built-in excuse to relapse were the primary reasons given by treatment clients for saying they had a disease even when they believed wholeheartedly that it was not true. Many substance abusers embrace any excuse to be insincere and abdicate responsibility for themselves, even if they know in their heart it's a lie.

A Disastrous Mistake

In a recent Gallup poll [as of 2003], 90 percent of people surveyed believe that alcoholism is a disease. Most argue that because the American Medical Association (AMA) has proclaimed alcoholism a disease, the idea is without reproach. But the fact is that the AMA made this determination in the absence of empirical evidence. After reviewing the history of the decision, it would not be unreasonable to suggest that the AMA has been pursuing its own agenda in the face of evidence negating the validity of alcoholism. While the AMA has made extraordinary contributions in the mental health field, it is not outside the box. The AMA is a part of the capitalist paradigm that is necessary for our society to function. The promulgation of the disease concept, in conjunction with AMA approval, has created a multi-billion dollar treatment industry that contributes billions to the health care industry. But even with the AMA's lofty status, mistakes in classifications can and have resulted in disastrous consequence. . . .

Failure of Existing Treatment Programs

Estimates among the general population indicate that 6–12% have substance abuse problems. The population of substance abusers has slowly increased since the 1930's coinciding with the spread of the disease concept and governmental interference in individual freedoms. What it is interesting that since the 70's the percentage of substance abuse population has increased dramatically, just like the popularity and prevalence of the drug treatment industry. The question is: if the multi-billion dollar war on drugs and the multi-billion dollar treatment industry have been growing, why does the drug problem continue to get worse?

Irrefutable empirical evidence has shown that organizations and institutions that promote, and adhere to, the disease concept, fail when trying to help people with substance abuse problems. Alcoholics Anonymous has successfully promoted itself as the only hope for alcohol abusers. The public perception is that Alcoholics Anonymous works, but the reality is something completely different.

In 65 years Alcoholics Anonymous has become a part of our social structure. Its tenets have been used by the medical establishment to diagnose patients with alcoholism while simultaneously giving birth to dozens of spin-off anonymous meetings. Its most outstanding accomplishment has been successfully promoting a fictitious disease, as fact, and to be absorbed into the very fabric of our society. But while Alcoholics Anonymous has accomplished the unthinkable, its accomplishments have damaged the society. Although its intentions are synonymous with help, the organization's lies and manipulations have damaged society as a whole, costing taxpayers billions of dollars and costing families the lives of their loved ones. . . .

In 1990, the Alcoholic's Anonymous General Services Office or AA GSO, the governing organization overseeing all "autonomous" meetings, published an internal memo for the employees of its offices. It was an analysis of a survey period between 1977 and 1989. The results were in absolute contrast to the public perception of AA. "After just one month in the Fellowship, 81 percent of the new members have already dropped out. After three months, 90 percent have left, and a full 95 percent have disappeared inside one year!" (Kolenda

2003 Golden Text Publishing Company). That means that in under a year, 95 percent of the people seeking from AA leave the program. While this only speaks for attendance, it has further implications. AA surveyors do not include dropouts in their sobriety statistics, which is a deceptive, if not outright dishonest, practice. Using the AA GSO statistics, and including the program dropouts, the success rate of AA as a whole "the total averages of sobriety for the total AA membership become 3.7 percent for one year [of sobriety], and 2.5 percent over five years" (Kolenda, 2003, Golden Text Publishing Company). It's important to understand that 95 percent of all substance abuse treatment centers in the United States are 12-step based programs. Thus, the failures of AA are also the failures of treatment.

Taking Personal Responsibility

Repeated studies have shown that the average person, who could be diagnosed with a substance abuse problem, will discontinue use *on their own* 20 to 30 percent of the time. But those who are exposed to AA and treatment and who are taught the disease concept have a drastically decreased chance of achieving sobriety. While treatment professionals are aware of program failure, governing organizations support and promote the adoption of 12-step tenets into treatment programs for substance abusers. Families pay tens of thousands of dollars to help their loved ones only to place them in programs that follow guidelines of another falling program. Any program based on a program that fails will inevitably fail. For most, 12-step has become synonymous with failure.

In contrast, programs that teach control and choice are far more successful than programs that teach the disease concept. While conventional treatment methods result in a 3 percent success rate after five years, programs that do not teach the disease concept, and instead teach choice, have success rates of 86 percent after five and even 10 years.

In conclusion, after reviewing the available research from both sides of the debate, the belief in the disease of alcoholism creates the existence of the disease. Organizations and institutions that promote the disease concept are, in many cases, doing irreparable harm to the individual and performing a disservice to the population as a whole. Geneticists are aware that a predisposition does not dictate subsequent behavior, and treatment professionals are aware that the programs they offer fail. It is an outright injustice when faced with the facts. Stripping human beings of their ability to choose is damaging, whereas giving them back the power of their own volition is essential for recovery. Alcoholism is a choice, not a disease.

"The earlier one drinks in adolescence, the greater the likelihood that he or she will develop alcoholism."

Youth Drinking Leads to Alcoholism

Ting-Kai Li

New research shows that youth is the stage in life in which alcoholism is most likely to begin, maintains Ting-Kai Li in the following viewpoint. He says that the younger an adolescent is when he or she begins drinking, the more likely that he or she will develop alcoholism. In light of such research, Li argues that the best approach to reducing the numerous public health problems related to alcohol use is to focus on preventing and treating youth alcohol consumption. Li is director of the National Institute on Alcohol Abuse and Alcoholism, the lead federal agency for study of alcohol and health.

As you read, consider the following questions:

1. By what age are most cases of alcoholism established, as stated by Li?
2. According to the author, what are the annual costs to U.S. society of alcohol misuse?

Ting-Kai Li, "Statement before the House and Senate Appropriations Subcommittee," 2005 *President's Budget Request for NIAAA*, April 8, 2004.

3. What type of shift in alcoholism research does Li advocate in light of recent findings connecting youth drinking with alcoholism?

As the recent [2003] NIAAA [National Institute on Alcohol Abuse and Alcoholism] National Epidemiologic Survey on Alcohol and Related Conditions (NESARC) has shown, most cases of alcoholism are established by age 25, beginning as early as age 18. These new results, which are corroborated by [other] studies ... call for a major refocusing of research on youth as the most important target for preventing alcohol abuse and alcoholism on a public-health scale. We now know that youth and adolescence are the critical window of opportunity. The earlier one drinks in adolescence, the greater the likelihood that he or she will develop alcoholism.

Alcohol-Related Health Problems

The public-health implications of preventing alcoholism before it becomes established in youth are large, given the magnitude of alcohol misuse and its consequences. The 2002 report of the World Health Organization ranks alcohol third as a preventable risk factor for premature death in developed nations. Only tobacco and cholesterol are greater risk factors.

In the U.S., almost 18 million American adults met the clinical diagnostic criteria for alcohol abuse or alcohol dependence in 2002. Annual costs to U.S. society of the consequences of alcohol misuse are about $185 billion.

Heavy alcohol use in the American military is on the rise, with more than 19 percent of male personnel and more than 5 percent of female personnel reporting heavy use (The Department of Defense defined heavy drinking as five or more drinks on one occasion, at least once a week, in its survey). This pattern of drinking is hazardous to the health and welfare of the individual, the family, and society. In the general population of the U.S., alcohol-related illness and injury account for at least 8 percent of all emergency-room visits.

Alcohol Use by Youth

Alcohol is the primary psychoactive substance of abuse by American children. As the NIAAA FY [Fiscal Year] 2005 Congressional Budget Justification notes, 78 percent of 12th graders, 67 percent of 10th graders, and 47 percent of 8th graders have used alcohol.

The same source of those statistics, the National Institute on Drug Abuse's *Monitoring the Future* survey, also indicates that youth who report having been drunk at least once include 62 percent of 12th graders, 44 percent of 10th graders, and 21 percent of 8th graders. Roughly half of those percentages say that they drank heavily—five or more drinks in a row in the past 2 weeks.

The NESARC data show that most cases of addiction, not only to alcohol, but also to other drugs of abuse, first occur in youth, after which new cases drop off sharply. The same research shows that, by comparison, new cases of depression do not follow this trajectory, instead continuing to rise after adulthood.

Refocusing the Research

The new finding that youth is the stage of life during which alcoholism is most likely to begin calls for a shift in the emphasis of our research. By focusing even more strongly than we currently do on developing strategies to prevent the onset of alcoholism in this population, we have the potential to dramatically reduce, overall, the occurrence of this common disease.

Likewise, shifting the focus of our medication development program to the early stages of the disease stands to improve the effectiveness of treatment. As with most diseases, early treatment for alcoholism could prevent a host of problems, including the medical sequelae of [condition resulting from] heavy alcohol use, which are estimated to cost $18.9 billion annually.

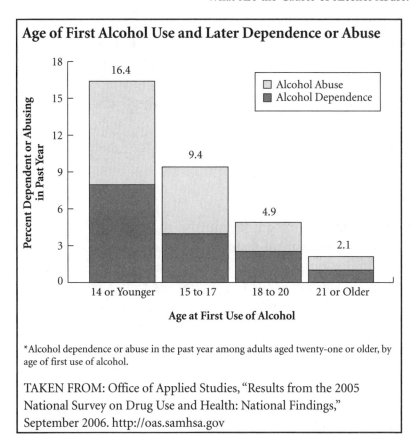

Age of First Alcohol Use and Later Dependence or Abuse

*Alcohol dependence or abuse in the past year among adults aged twenty-one or older, by age of first use of alcohol.

TAKEN FROM: Office of Applied Studies, "Results from the 2005 National Survey on Drug Use and Health: National Findings," September 2006. http://oas.samhsa.gov

Studies show that a combination of factors underlie drinking behaviors. Environmental factors—family and peers, for example—are the dominating influences on whether or not an individual first uses alcohol. Personality and temperament also influence the decision to begin drinking. These factors have a profound effect on youth.

Whether or not drinking continues also is influenced by differences, from individual to individual, in the pharmacological effects (activities of genes, proteins, and metabolic products) that come into play once drinking has begun. When drinking progresses to alcoholism, alcohol's pharmacological effects will have become the dominant influence on drinking behavior.

Identifying the pharmacological effects of alcohol is essential to our ability to design effective prevention and treatment strategies for youth. In childhood and adolescence, the pharmacological effects of alcohol are occurring at a time of rapid structural and physiological change in the brain. One of the major questions before us is how alcohol's pharmacological effects work in ways that specifically promote alcoholism during this vulnerable time of life. . . .

Actions Underway

Our current research on drinking by youth includes studies of the neurobiological mechanisms of adolescent alcohol abuse; an initiative on preventing alcohol-related problems among college students; expanded testing of preventive interventions, from rural children to children in urban, diverse neighborhoods; and an initiative that is examining risk factors and testing community-based, longitudinal prevention programs among children in rural and small urban areas . . .

In addition to our research, we conduct outreach programs for youth. The Leadership to Keep Children Alcohol-Free has recruited 33 governors' spouses to spearhead a national prevention campaign. The Task Force on College Drinking has brought together university presidents and researchers, and is making headway in efforts to reduce drinking by college students and in evaluating those efforts.

The Larger Picture

Alcohol abuse and alcoholism often result in behavioral outcomes such as property damage, legal problems, disrupted family lives, and derailed academic pursuits and professional careers. But its consequences also include medical sequelae. With prolonged, heavy use, it can act as a toxin, damaging virtually any organ in the body. For example, alcohol is a leading cause of liver cirrhosis and contributes to some kinds of cancer. Approximately 77 percent of the annual $185 billion cost of alcohol misuse is health-related, generated by medical consequences and lost productivity associated with illness or death.

Research leading to effective strategies for preventing and treating alcoholism early in life, when it is most likely to begin, can help avert many other costly problems. While we will increase our research on drinking by youth, we will continue our studies of the many other facets of alcohol use, such as fetal alcohol syndrome, as well as our research on the apparent protective effect of moderate drinking against certain chronic diseases.

> *"In a 'wet culture' where young people are early socialized to drinking, they . . . learn how to drink moderately."*

In Most Cultures, Youth Drinking Does Not Lead to Alcoholism

Dwight Heath

In the following viewpoint, Dwight Heath maintains that the correlation between youth drinking and alcoholism exists only in the United States, where adults try to prevent youth under age twenty-one from consuming alcohol. The problem with such a policy is that American youth are not taught how to drink responsibly, says Heath, and thus they often do end up abusing alcohol. In his opinion, the best way to reduce alcohol-related problems is to socialize youth to alcohol at an early age. Heath is a professor of anthropology at Brown University in Rhode Island.

As you read, consider the following questions:

1. How do Orthodox Jews approach the issue of youth drinking, according to Heath?

2. Rather than viewing drinking as a risky act, what do children who drink with their families learn about alcohol, in the author's opinion?

3. In Heath's opinion, what kind of problems result from the "just-say-no" approach?

Newspapers and magazines in the United States have just been crowded with another gloomy piece of news about alcohol. The press-release that triggered this most recent wave of ominous predictions grew out of a research project (sponsored by National Institute on Alcohol Abuse and Alcoholism) concerning the correlation between "age-of-onset" and alcoholism. In simplest terms, investigators discovered that those individuals who started drinking at an early age were more likely to become alcoholics later in life to a statistically significant degree.

Correlation Does Not Mean Causation

One need not be a scientist to realize that correlation often has little to do with causation, but most journalists wrote as if this were dramatic proof of the highly addictive quality of alcohol, and of the dangers of drinking on the part of anyone under 21 years of age. However, to anyone who has paid attention to life in contemporary Europe where children are frequently introduced to drinking at an early age and where rates of dependency tend to be quite low the finding seems counterintuitive. Similarly, when one thinks of Orthodox Jews anywhere in the world it is difficult to reconcile their famously low rates of drinking problems with the fact that male infants are given wine on the occasion of their circumcision (on the 8th day of life), and men, women, and children all drink at least twice a week to celebrate the beginning and end of the Sabbath.

In view of the vast panorama of human experience, the fateful findings about early drinking are in fact not only

Problems with Unsupervised Drinking

The current drinking age fosters binge drinking on college campus' and dangerous behaviors by teens who resort to unsupervised partying because they are considered not responsible enough to handle alcohol. Large numbers of teens drink despite the current law. Some say that it is easier for kids to get drugs than it is to obtain alcohol. We must move to a more responsible system which includes parents educating their children and young adults on the dangers of drunk driving and alcohol abuse.

Jeff Rainforth, "Issues,"
2005–2006. www.rainforth4congress.org.

counter-intuitive but would be factually wrong in most of the world. However, in the contemporary US, there is little question that the findings are correct, and, when one thinks about it for a while, quite logical.

The Problem with Protecting Children from Alcohol

The difference is that part of the way in which members of the new temperance movement have tried to "protect American children from alcohol" has obviously been counterproductive. Given a setting where it is deviant (or even illegal) to drink at an early age, it is no surprise that those who do so are precisely those who choose to act in deviant, illegal, or other risky ways. By the same token, moderate individuals who are willing to conform to norms, obey the laws, and minimize risks are those most likely to defer drinking until later. The anti-drink constituency have succeeded in structuring the situation in such a way that the fateful outcome ("early drinking results in drinking problems") is all but inevitable!

By contrast, in most parts of the world, beverage alcohol has not been endowed with a mystical aura of "forbidden fruit" in such a way that drinking it is expected by young people to demonstrate their maturity, to make them more powerful or sexy or dynamic or sociable. Where children are not "protected from alcohol," they show no need of such protection. They learn to drink, usually at home and among their families. Drinking is a wholesome and enjoyable part of everyday life, rather than a risky act which they should hide from their elders, and learn from their ill-informed and inexperienced peers.

As an anthropologist, I often deal with patterns of small, isolated, or even tribal populations whose exotic patterns of belief and behaviour would be impractical in a modern urban setting in the industrial or post-industrial world. But this is not such a case. Some of the best illustrations of my point are the middle-class cultures of contemporary France, Italy, and Spain (among many others). It is in those well-studied and heavily documented contexts that I have repeatedly demonstrated, using their own official statistics, that the occurrence of so-called "alcohol-related problems" (whether physiological, psychological, social relational, economic, or other) is inversely related to both "age-of-onset" and to average per-capita consumption.

As you know, this is just the opposite of what is claimed by the World Health Organization, US [United States] National Institute on Alcohol Abuse and Alcoholism, and other organizations and individuals that are primarily concerned with restricting or curtailing availability as a public health policy.

Importance of Socialization to Drinking

Incidentally, the same context that guarantees that early-onset drinkers be deviant and willing to flout the law, also guarantees that they will often do so surreptitiously, drinking too much and/or too fast, among peers who lack knowledge about the specific risks of drunkenness or chemical harm, and who may be reluctant to summon adults in the event that an acute problem should occur. Here again, it is the "just-say-no" approach that makes for problems rather than reducing the potential for harm.

In a "wet culture" where young people are early socialized to drinking, they simultaneously learn how to drink moderately, how and why to avoid drunkenness, not to expect magical transformations from drink, and to view excesses as inappropriate and illustrative of weakness (generally the opposite of what supposedly "protected" youths in the US learn).

In short, the "early onset" theory is accurate but only in those few parts of the world in which the legal and normative system makes it so. In the rest of the world, the opposite is the case!. . .

How ironic it is that an illogical scientific finding should hold, if only because an illogical legal context structures the situation in a way that assures that perverse outcome.

Periodical Bibliography

The following articles have been selected to supplement the diverse views presented in this chapter.

Alcoholism & Drug Abuse Weekly	"Alcohol Advertising in Magazines Continues to Overexpose Youth," April 18, 2005.
Barbara Isaacs	"Loosening the Grip of Addiction," *Lexington Herald-Leader*, December 2005.
Carolyn Marshall	"Drinks with Youth Appeal Draw Growing Opposition," *New York Times*, April 13, 2007.
Michael Craig Miller	"Addiction: How to Break the Chain," *Newsweek*, December 12, 2005.
John P. Nelson	"Advertising, Alcohol, and Youth: Is the Alcoholic Beverage Industry Targeting Minors with Magazine Ads?" *Regulation*, Summer 2005.
Stanton Peele	"The Surprising Truth About Addiction: More People Quit Addictions than Maintain Them, and They Do So On Their Own. That's Not to Say It Happens Overnight," *Psychology Today*, May 1, 2004.
Robert Preidt	"Underage Drinking Nets Alcohol Industry Billions," *HealthDay*, May 2006.
USA Today	"Shame, Not Guilt Linked to Addiction," October 2005.
Karen Springen and Barbara Kantrowitz	"Alcohol's Deadly Triple Threat," *Newsweek*, May 2004.
National Women's Health Report	"Substance Abuse, Addiction & Women," December 1, 2006.
Mark Warmat	"One Day at a Time," *Journal of the American Academy of Physicians Assistants*, January 2005.
Jill Westfall	"Society Doesn't See Addiction as a Disease: Sisters Are Dying," *Essence*, October 1, 2004.

VIEWPOINTS® SERIES

CHAPTER 4

What Measures Should Be Taken to Reduce Alcohol-Related Problems?

Chapter Preface

One of the most serious alcohol-related problems in the United States is drunk driving. The National Transportation Safety Board estimates that approximately 40 percent of the country's highway deaths are alcohol-related. In an effort to reduce alcohol-related accidents, a 2000 federal law was passed making it illegal to drive with a blood alcohol content (BAC) over .08. BAC laws are just one way that the United States and other countries attempt to reduce alcohol-related problems in society. However, BAC laws and other measures also face widespread criticism.

There are many who support .08 BAC laws. The National Highway Transportation Safety Administration (NHTSA) states: "At .08 BAC, all drivers, even experienced drinkers, show impairment in driving ability. For the great majority, there is serious deterioration in driving performance at .08 BAC." A number of studies conducted by the administration supports its position that .08 laws help reduce drunk driving-related roadway accidents. Mothers Against Drunk Driving (MADD) agrees. According to MADD, "At .08 BAC any driver is a dangerous threat on the road." The organization insists that at .08, all of the basic driving skills such as braking, steering, and response time are affected, and the risk of a fatal crash increases significantly. It states, ".08 BAC is a proven effective measure to reduce alcohol-related traffic deaths. Studies have shown a 6 to 8 percent reduction in alcohol-related traffic deaths in states following the passage of .08 BAC."

However, .08 BAC laws also have many critics. Policy analyst at the Cato Institute Charles V. Peña argues that the NHTSA and MADD have used unsound statistics to back up their arguments for .08 BAC laws. He states: "The more evidence that comes in from states that have gone to a .08% BAC standard, the weaker the case is for .08. In a fair fight of facts, the argument for .08% BAC lost again and again," The organization GetMADD is opposed to any BAC laws. It argues, "Different people experience different levels of impairment at the same BAC levels." The organization believes that rather than testing for BAC levels, drunk driving arrests should be based on a driver's behavior. Police should issue DWI [driving while impaired] tickets to drivers who drive erratically and who hit fixed objects.

As the following chapter shows, people use many different measures such as .08 BAC laws in the United States—in an effort to reduce the problems caused by alcohol. However there is widespread disagreement over the wisdom and effectiveness of these various policies.

> "The public health goal . . . [should be]
> to minimize the harm caused by drink-
> ing."

Society Should Focus on Reducing the Negative Impacts of Alcohol

World Health Organization

Alcohol consumption creates many economic and social costs, maintains the World Health Organization (WHO) in the following viewpoint. According to WHO, alcohol use contributes to workplace accidents and lower productivity, poverty, domestic violence, and impairs an individual's ability to function as part of a family. The organization advises that governments worldwide take action to reduce these numerous harms caused by drinking. WHO is a specialized agency of the United Nations that works to help improve the health of people around the world.

As you read, consider the following questions:

1. How does heavy drinking lower workplace productivity, as explained by the author?

World Health Organization, *Global Status Report on Alcohol 2004*, Geneva: World Health Organization, Department of Mental Health and Substance Abuse, 2004. Copyright © World Health Organization (WHO). Reproduced by permission.

2. According to WHO, what kind of adverse economic effects does a heavy drinker suffer?

3. In reducing alcohol-related harm, what two different dimensions of consumption should be addressed, according to the author?

A lcohol consumption is linked to many harmful consequences for the individual drinker, the drinker's immediate environment and society as a whole. Such social consequences as traffic accidents, workplace-related problems, family and domestic problems, and interpersonal violence have been receiving more public or research attention in recent years [as of 2004], indicating a growing interest in a broader concept of alcohol-related consequences. On the other hand, however, social consequences affect individuals other than the drinker e.g. passengers involved in traffic casualties, or family members affected by failure to fulfill social role obligations, or incidences of violence in the family. Ultimately, however, these events have an impact on society as a whole insofar as they affect economic productivity or require the attention and resources of the criminal justice or health care system, or of other social institutions. . . .

Alcohol Consumption and the Workplace

Heavy drinking at the workplace may potentially lower productivity. Sickness absence associated with harmful use of alcohol and alcohol dependence entails a substantial cost to employees and social security systems. There is ample evidence that people with alcohol dependence and problem drinkers have higher rates of sickness absence than other employees. . . .

Some examples may highlight the extent to which alcohol affects work performance. It has been estimated that 30% of absenteeism and workplace accidents in Costa Rica were caused by alcohol dependence. According to industry association sources from India, 15% to 20% of absenteeism and 40%

of accidents at work are due to alcohol consumption. A study by the Department of Hygiene and Industrial Safety in three factories in La Paz, Bolivia found that 7.3% of absenteeism in the first two days of the work week and 1.2% of work-related accidents were directly related to the consumption of alcohol. It has been estimated that 20–22% of work-related accidents in Chile have a direct or indirect relationship with recent alcohol use. In a study of patients who required hospitalization for severe work-related accidents, it was found that 15% reported recent use of alcohol. It has been reported that in Latvia, alcoholism has had adverse impacts on productivity in the workplace and increased absenteeism. No figures have been published on the extent of absenteeism due to excessive alcohol use. It is estimated that drinking and alcoholism have reduced labour productivity by some 10%. A recent survey conducted in the United States of America found that farm residents who drank more frequently had significantly higher farm work injury incidence rates (3.35 per 10,000 person-days of observation) than others who consumed less frequently (1.94 injuries per 10,000 person-days). . . .

Alcohol Consumption and the Family

It is well established that drinking can severely impair the individual's functioning in various social roles. Alcohol misuse is associated with many negative consequences both for the drinker's partner as well as the children. Maternal alcohol consumption during pregnancy can result in fetal alcohol syndrome in children, and parental drinking is correlated with child abuse and impacts a child's environment in many social, psychological and economic ways. Drinking can impair performance as a parent, as a spouse or partner, and as a contributor to household functioning. There are also other aspects of drinking which may impair functioning as a family member. In many societies, drinking may be carried out primarily outside the family and the home. In this circumstance, time spent while drinking often competes with the time needed to carry on family life. Drinking also costs money and can impact upon resources particularly of a poor family, leaving other family members destitute. Also, it is worth noting that specific intoxicated events can also have lasting consequences, through home accidents and family violence. A recent paper ... suggests that adverse child health effects of alcohol use are primarily through two distal determinants (indirect effects)—forgone household disposable income and caretakers' time for childcare. Diversion of scant economic resources for alcohol use that could have otherwise been used for seeking health care, may lead to self-care or delay in seeking health care. The other potential ways by which alcohol use can reduce the household income are through morbidity associated with the drinking habit among the consuming individuals, resulting in increase in medical expenditures and loss of income due to lost wages, and, sometimes, resulting in the premature death of sole wage earners in a household.

Implicit in the habitual drinker's potential impact on family life is the fact that the drinking and its consequences can result in substantial mental health problems of family members. Such effects, though potentially common, are not often documented. Some insight into this issue can be gained from interviews with members of Al-Anon, a companion organization to Alcoholic Anonymous for spouses and family members of people with alcohol dependence. In interviews with 45 Al-Anon members in Mexico (82% of them had husbands who were alcohol-dependent), 73% reported feelings of anxiety, fear, and depression; 62% reported physical or verbal aggression by the spouse toward the family; and 31% reported family disintegration with serious problems involving money and the children.

The effects of men's drinking on other members of the family is often particularly on women in their roles as mothers or wives of drinkers. The risks include violence, HIV [hu-

Alcohol's Impact on American Society

- In 2002, about 18 million adults in the US met diagnostic criteria for alcohol disorders.

- More than one-half of American adults have a close family member who is an alcoholic or has abused alcohol.

- Research was conducted in 1998 to determine the total cost attributable to the consequences of underage drinking. The cost was more than $58 billion per year, based on year 2000 dollars.

- In 1998, the estimated productivity loss for workers with past or current alcoholism was $86.4 billion. Productivity losses were greatest for males who initiated drinking before age 15.

- In a survey of 18- to 24-year-old current drinkers who failed to complete high school, nearly 60% had begun to drink before age 16.

- Long-term heavy alcohol use is the leading cause of illness and death from liver disease in the U.S.

- Alcohol is implicated in more than 100,000 deaths annually.

Leadership to Keep Children Alcohol Free,
"How Does Alcohol Affect the World of a Child?"
March 2005. www.alcoholfreechildren.org.

man immunodeficiency virus] infection, and an increased burden in their role of economic providers. In a paper that looked at alcohol and alcohol-related problems facing women in Lesotho, it was noted that as in many other developing countries, the cultural position of women in Lesotho facilitates a vicious circle in which women are at one time brewers of alcohol, then sellers, then become excessive consumers due to the problems created by their drinking husbands.

Alcohol and Poverty

The economic consequences of expenditures on alcohol are significant especially in high poverty areas. Besides money spent on alcohol, a heavy drinker also suffers other adverse economic effects. These include lowered wages (because of missed work and decreased efficiency on the job), lost employment opportunities, increased medical expenses for illness and accidents, legal cost of drink-related offences, and decreased eligibility of loans. A recent study conducted in 11 districts in Sri Lanka examining the link between alcohol and poverty found that 7% of men said that their alcohol expenditure was greater than their income. Though a relatively small percentage, this is still a worrying statistic for the families concerned and for those interested in helping the worst-off families.

Alcohol and Domestic Violence

Research has found that alcohol is present in a substantial number of domestic violence accidents. The most common pattern is drinking by both offender and victim. Alcohol has been shown to be a significant risk factor for husband-to-wife violence. Studies have shown that the relationship between alcohol and domestic violence is complex.

Drinking frequently has been associated with intrafamily violence. Reviews have found that excessive alcohol use is a strong and consistent correlate of marital violence, but that violence rates vary based on research designs, methodologies, and samples. Therefore, the role of alcohol remains unclear. Studies based on interviews with abused wives tend to report higher proportions of alcohol involvement than do general population studies or police samples. In a study examining episodes of domestic violence reported to the police in Zurich, Switzerland, evidence of alcohol involvement was found in 40% of the investigated situations. Police officers thus believed there was a clear link between alcohol and violence in at least 26% of the cases studied.

Regarding partner violence, research evidence indicates that it is more strongly associated with heavy drinking, whether usual or occasional, than is non-partner violence, and conflicts as to whether drinking by the victim makes violent acts by a partner more likely. That alcohol consumption has a stronger association with partner violence than with nonpartner violence may be a matter of access, with partners having more contact and thus more opportunities for violent encounters. Studies also report an association between drinking patterns and intimate partner violence; excessive drinkers and alcohol-dependent individuals are more likely to act violently toward their intimate partners.

To give some examples from the literature, a study conducted in Nigeria showed a strong association between domestic violence and alcohol use. Alcohol use was involved in 51% of the cases in which a husband stabbed a wife. In a 1998 cross-sectional study of violence against women undertaken in three provinces in South Africa, it was found that domestic violence was significantly positively associated with the women drinking alcohol and conflict over the partner's drinking.

In a 2000–2001 survey of 5,109 women of reproductive age in the Rakai District of Uganda, it was found that the strength of the association between alcohol consumption and domestic violence was particularly noteworthy. Women whose partners frequently or always consumed alcohol before having sex faced risks of domestic violence almost five times higher than those whose partners never drank before having sex. Of women who recently experienced domestic violence, 52% reported that their partner had consumed alcohol and 27% reported that their partners had frequently consumed alcohol. This finding supports the conclusion that alcohol may play a direct precipitating role in domestic violence.

In a study of 180 women seeking prenatal care in rural South India, it was found that 20% of the women reported domestic violence and 94.5% of these women identified their husbands as the aggressors. The husband's alcohol use was a significant risk factor for domestic violence. The role of alcohol in domestic violence is also cited in another Indian study which found that 33% of spouse-abusing husbands were using alcohol. Of these 15% were occasional, 45% frequent and about 40% were daily users of alcohol. More than half of the spousal abuse took place during the period of intoxication. A cross-sectional study of a random sample of 275 women in Barranquilla, Colombia, found that habitual alcohol consumption in the women and in the spouses were factors associated with marital violence.

It has been suggested that because alcohol-dependent individuals are intoxicated more frequently than non-dependent individuals, the observed association between spousal abuse and intoxication may occur simply by chance. In addition, most instances of spouse abuse occur in the absence of alcohol intoxication, suggesting the need to understand better the processes through which some episodes escalate into violence. Although many studies have found that alcohol use is associated with intimate partner violence, the nature of the association needs to be clarified.

In conclusion, however, there is little doubt that alcohol consumption is associated with many social consequences. The available data on consequences to the direct social and personal environment from short-term as well as long-term use of alcohol are sparse. Much more research into this issue would be required to obtain standard measures or data that would allow quantification of these consequences in a meaningful and comparable manner.

Economic and Social Costs of Alcohol Use

There is a strong interest in many countries regarding the development of scientifically valid, credible estimates of the economic costs of alcohol use (and use of other psychoactive substance use like tobacco and drugs). It is a well established fact that the use of alcohol entails a large number of adverse consequences in such widely differing areas as physical and mental health, traffic safety, violence, and labour productivity. There has been much effort in the past three decades [between 1974 and 2004] in attempting to estimate these costs and recent investigations have suggested that they account annually for a substantial part of the Gross Domestic Product of industrialized countries. . . .

Relatively few countries have attempted to estimate the costs of alcohol use. Estimating the costs of alcohol consumption encounters problems over availability of data as well as methodological difficulties. However, the fact that studies carried out in different countries using a variety of approaches and methods all seem to lead to convergent results is a positive indication that results are valid. In all cases, there is confirmation that alcohol consumption imposes significant damage on society. . . .

Need to Minimize the Harm Caused by Alcohol

Alcohol is not an ordinary commodity. While it carries connotations of pleasure and sociability in the minds of many, harmful consequences of its use are diverse and widespread. As documented in this report, globally, alcohol problems exert an enormous toll on the lives and communities of many nations, especially those in the developing world. Research has shown that when extrapolating from historical trends, the role of alcohol as a major factor in the burden of disease will be increasing in the future. Particularly worrying trends are the increases in average volume of drinking predicted for the most populous regions of the world (e.g. in China and India) and the emerging trend of more harmful and risky patterns in drinking especially among young people.

A global perspective on alcohol policy needs to acknowledge and take into account the characteristics, effects and consequences of alcohol use in different societies, and yet to focus and act on the public health goal which is to minimize the harm caused by drinking. Alcohol-related burden is linked to at least two different dimensions of consumption: average volume and patterns of drinking. Thus, in order to avoid or reduce burden, both dimensions should be taken into consideration. In other words, one may reduce the burden by decreasing the average volume of alcohol consumed or by shifting patterns of drinking to less harmful patterns. . . .

To effectively reduce the level of harmful social and health consequences from alcohol use requires much preparation and planning. It is now the responsibility of governments worldwide and concerned citizens to encourage healthy debate and formulate effective public health-oriented countermeasures in order to minimize the harm caused by alcohol use.

> *"Ignoring health and pleasure benefits, while referring only to the danger and harm associated with alcohol, may delay—even permanently impair—people's ability to adopt sensible and pleasurable drinking practices."*

Society Should Celebrate the Positive Aspects of Alcohol

Stanton Peele

In the following viewpoint Stanton Peele argues that in cultures around the world, alcohol provides pleasure and enhances people's well-being. Peele is critical of public health organization policies that focus only on alcohol's dangers, while ignoring these benefits. He believes that alcohol policies, particularly education of youth, will be more effective if they recognize the positive aspects of alcohol consumption. Peele is a psychologist and author of numerous books and articles on the subject of alcoholism and addiction.

Stanton Peele, "Drinking Education: Minimizing Negatives or Optimizing Potential?" in *Corporate Social Responsibility and Alcohol*. Danvers, MA: Routledge, 2005, pp. 63–74. Copyright © 2005 by International Center for Alcohol Policies. Republished with permission of Routledge, an imprint of Taylor & Francis Group, conveyed through Copyright Clearance Center, Inc.

As you read, consider the following questions:

1. As explained by the author, what is the attitude toward drinking in Spain?

2. According to Peele, by the late 1990s, why had it become a dubious public health proposition to try to eliminate drinking in some countries?

3. In the author's opinion, in the United States, how effective is current youth education on alcohol use?

Views of alcohol vary for different individuals, cultures, and epochs. In particular, some people and societies view mild imbibing as a joyous experience, while others view alcohol as evil. That images of alcohol vary, even sometimes in the same place and for the same person, is captured in a popular historical anecdote:

> A Congressman was once asked by a constituent to explain his attitude towards whiskey. "If you mean the demon drink that poisons the mind, pollutes the body, desecrates family life and inflames sinners, then I'm against it," the Congressman said. "But if you mean the elixir of Christmas cheer, the shield against winter chill, the taxable potion that puts needed funds into public coffers to comfort little crippled children, then I'm for it. This is my position. and I will not compromise."

Parts of society in the United States—and, increasingly, the public health bodies worldwide—emphasize exclusively the danger and drawbacks of consuming alcohol, although none suggests prohibiting the substance. Yet, the way in which we conceive of the drinking experience strongly influences the nature of that experience, often in a self-fulfilling way. Thus, ignoring health and pleasure benefits, while referring only to the danger and harm associated with alcohol, may delay—even permanently impair—people's ability to adopt sensible and pleasurable drinking practices. This [viewpoint] ... describes an approach using positive models of drinking, emphasizing the pleasure it can provide.

The Pleasure of Alcohol

Some cultures and people seem to view alcohol much more positively than Americans do currently [as of 2005]. Throughout history there have been unabashed paeans to beverage alcohol, often in musical form:

A good wine is to be praised above all other things ...

Whoever wants to drink as much as I

Will also be made happy by this wine.

(Orlando Lassus [1532–1594], *Ein Guter Wein*)

In *Drinking Occasions: Comparative Perspectives on Alcohol and Culture*, [researcher] Dwight Heath notes about contemporary Spain, "[Alcoholic beverages] have always been the major social lubricant and a source of conviviality and sociability." Alcohol is consumed throughout the day, virtually every day; it is thought of as an essential pleasure. Yet, drunkenness and misbehavior when drinking are strongly disapproved of. This attitude toward and style of drinking is traditional throughout Mediterranean cultures.

The intense experience of pleasure with alcohol consumption is common, even in English-speaking cultures. Psychologist Geoff Lowe reviewed data from the Mass-Observation Archive at the University of Sussex, which has assessed the lives, views, and feelings of ordinary British people for 50 years. In 1993, Mass-Observation respondents were asked to write about pleasure and good times. Many discussed their drinking experiences, including the following two respondents. A 35-year-old female wrote:

Good wine can make me feel orgasmic. The nose, taste, and glow one gets can be overwhelming. I have occasionally had wine so delicious it has almost brought tears to my eyes. The ability to taste different spices, fruits, flowers, herbs within one glass of wine differentiates good wines to bad

159

wines for me, and a good wine requires time and thought to be enjoyed fully. However it is not for me, a thing to be deeply discussed and analysed as to what the definitive taste or nose is, but something to be slowly explored and quietly enjoyed. If I were to be marooned on a desert island I would have a good case of wine as my luxury (plus a corkscrew and a large glass!).

A 42-year-old male stated:

I am sitting outside a cottage/farmhouse in the evening somewhere in France (or maybe anywhere else in southern Europe) on a warm evening. It's a rural area—there is no traffic noise, no dogs barking, nobody asking me to do things for them. I have a good novel and a glass of red wine. In the background the crickets are chirping. Perhaps I am sitting with my wife who is reading a book as well, or perhaps I am with a group of 6 male friends who I go cycling with every other year and we have been for a meal and some drinks in the local bar. This for me is probably the ultimate pleasure!. . .

A Worldwide Trend

Drinking pleasures were not limited to any one form of alcohol or to any particular age range of respondents. Worldwide, at least among European cultures, general population surveys uniformly identify pleasure as first among the effects of drinking. Respondents in surveys in the United States, Canada, and Sweden predominantly mention positive sensations and experiences associated with drinking (e.g., relaxation and sociability), with little mention of harm. In two Australian surveys, most respondents identified relaxation, stress reduction, and improved psychological well-being as benefits of drinking. In Finland, both student and general populations reported positive effects more often than negative. Lowe, analyzing the Mass-Observation Archive data together with surveys of adolescent drinkers and temporary abstainers, reported that people usually found drinking enjoyable. [Researchers B.C.]

Leigh and [A.W.] Stacy found among several groups of drinkers in the United States that, when asked about the effects of alcohol, drinkers list positive effects first and foremost.

Public Health Groups Place Drinking Harms Foremost

Although historically and cross-culturally drinking is experienced as pleasurable, contemporary public health organizations now focus exclusively on the dangers of alcohol. It is not possible to cite all the examples of this, but recent developments show acceleration in this trend and a particular focus on attacking the alcohol industry. At the 2001 Stockholm conference, organized by the World Health Organization's [WHO] Regional Office for Europe and focused especially on the young, Gro Harlem Brundtland, then the director-general of WHO, stated:

> Globally, 140 million people are suffering from alcohol dependence. Around the world, alcohol takes a heavy toll—damaging public and private life with countless traffic fatalities and injuries, home fires, drowning, suicides and violent crimes. But also debt problems, ruined careers, divorces, birth defects, and children with permanent emotional damage.... Data from across the world suggest that a culture of sporadic binge drinking among young people may now be increasing also in developing countries. While overall rates of adult per capita consumption are falling in many countries, young people are too often drinking excessive quantities of alcohol to intoxication in single drinking episodes.

WHO has now committed itself to an international fight against drinking with the specific goal of reducing alcohol consumption, particularly among the young.

Anti-Alcohol Efforts in the USA

The United States is especially noteworthy for its efforts to discourage young people's drinking. In 2002, the National

A Social and Psychological Tonic

The social and psychological benefits of alcohol can't be ignored. A drink before a meal can improve digestion or offer a soothing respite at the end of a stressful day; the occasional drink with friends can be a social tonic. These physical and psychic effects may contribute to health and wellbeing.

Harvard School of Public Health, "Alcohol," 2006.
www.hsph.harvard.edu.

Center on Addiction and Substance Abuse (CASA) at Columbia University published a report titled *Teen Tipplers: America's Underage Drinking Epidemic*. CASA cited data from a number of sources in alarming terms. In a press release that accompanied the release of the report, CASA's president Joseph Califano Jr. said that "underage drinking has reached epidemic proportions in America," adding that "this report is a clarion call for national mobilization to curb underage drinking". Also in 2002, the American Medical Association issued a report titled *Partner or Foe: The Alcohol Industry, Youth Alcohol Policies, and Alcohol Policy Strategies*. The goal of this report was to undercut all efforts to encourage moderate drinking on college campuses ([beer company] Anheuser-Busch's social norms program was targeted in particular) on the grounds that the industry profits by encouraging drinking of the heaviest consumers and by encouraging youthful drinking. . . .

Prohibition Would Be Harmful and Impractical

It seems evident that drinking will persist among young people, as well as among adults. The question is, how problematic will such drinking be for the young? Thus far, we have shown no ability to reduce the harmfulness of drinking among those aged under 30. This continued drinking by the young, often of a high-risk nature, should be viewed in the context where prohibition of alcohol, as a goal, has been rejected by Western (and most other) nations.

Total prohibition of alcohol is not considered a plausible goal in Western countries because consumers in them demand the right to consume alcohol. At the same time, beginning in the 1980s, the health benefits of consuming alcohol became clear. Primarily, moderate drinking reduces the risk, and occurrence, of coronary artery disease (CAD). Since, for most population groups in the United States and elsewhere in the Western world, CAD is the largest cause of death, this translates into lower mortality rates and greater life expectancy for moderate consumers of alcohol compared with abstainers. In addition to being a political and social impracticality, by the late 1990s, it thus became a dubious public health proposition to try to eliminate drinking in countries with high rates of CAD. In other words, more people would *lose* life years in those countries if alcohol consumption were suddenly to disappear than would gain from such prohibition.

Psychological Benefits

Furthermore, a steady stream of research has begun to identify potential—and in some cases fairly well established— *psychological* benefits from moderate drinking. According to a survey by [A] Peele and [researchers S.] Brodsky, these benefits include, in addition to positive feelings, the following:

> To a greater degree than either abstainers or heavy drinkers, moderate drinkers have been found to experience a sense of psychological, physical, and social well-being; elevated mood; reduced stress (under some circumstances); reduced psychopathology, particularly depression; enhanced sociability and social participation; and higher incomes and less work absence or disability. The elderly often have higher levels of in-

volvement and activity in association with moderate drinking, while often showing better-than-average cognitive functioning following long-term moderate alcohol consumption.

One area that has repeatedly shown positive findings in prospective research (that is, research where subjects are identified and then followed up throughout their life spans) is improved cognitive functioning. . . .

What Do Young People Learn About Alcohol?

At this point, at least in the United States, nearly all young people have been informed repeatedly of the harm that alcohol can cause. Among other forms of harm, they are very familiar with alcohol dependence and, in fact, often note symptoms of alcohol dependence in themselves. Very often, however, the only alternative they perceive is not to drink at all: like the alcoholic who alternates between avoiding booze and drinking excessively, young people often drink to excess when they do drink. [Researcher Henry] Wechsler and colleagues find that among college students an increase in abstinence, combined with an increase in frequent excess (binge) drinking, is in line with this dichotomy.

What Should Young People Learn About Alcohol?

Given that alcohol is ubiquitous in Western societies, it seems important (as well as accurate) to note its benefits along with its dangers. That is, moderate drinking increases longevity and can be psychologically beneficial for most drinkers. Learning these things implies the need to educate people in how to regulate their drinking. Indeed, even for high-school students in the United States, which alone among Western nations restricts legal drinking to those aged 21 years and older, there is ample opportunity to drink. Finally, given its likely presence throughout one's lifecycle, it seems worthwhile to inform the young that alcohol may be made an enjoyable part of life.

In addition to these points about personal pleasure, there are equivalent considerations concerning the social obligation for individuals to regulate their drinking. Even for those who drink excessively as youths, the goal should be to learn to drink moderately ... The concept of moderate drinking is both possible and beneficial; it is beneficial for the individual and for those around the individual as well as for society at large. In other words, people should learn as an ethical tenet that excessive drinking and antisocial behavior while drinking are wrong.

Who Should Teach Positive Drinking Practices?

None of the primary institutions that present models for alcohol consumption has a special interest in conveying the benefits of moderate drinking and individual responsibility. Public health advocates, for their part, emphasize the dangers of drinking, including its ability to produce dependence and cause people to lose personal control. School-based education programs frequently rely on recovering alcoholics to present antidrinking messages. Like latter-day temperance lecturers, they teach children to associate drinking with excess, drunkenness, and loss of control. This may partially explain why young people in the United States increasingly display such loss of control and other dependence symptoms. Alcohol producers and advertisers speak about drinking responsibly. But alcohol advertising traditionally associates consumption with prestige purchases, social and sexual success and excess (particularly for young males), and other images of personal power and assertiveness. These images do not encourage moderate drinking, but rather the opposite.

How Are We Doing in Teaching the Young to Drink?

The data indicate that the young are not being taught how to regulate their drinking or how to drink moderately. Rather, they continue to practice relatively risky drinking. According to [researcher M.] Plant, such risk-taking may be a part of youthful development, one that can never be eliminated. Nonetheless, some basis should be laid for encouraging the emergence of regulated, pleasurable, and sensible drinking. As well as accelerating the development of sensible drinking, such knowledge should increase adults' skills in drinking responsibly, increasing the proportion of consumers who behave constructively and drink healthily.

Education in sensible drinking is not being conducted. The Monitoring the Future survey measures students' attitudes toward drinking, as well as their actual drinking. In 2001, although 69% of high school seniors disapproved of taking one or two drinks nearly every day, fewer (63%) disapproved of taking five or six drinks once or twice each weekend. That is, they disapproved as much or more of the kind of drinking likely to prolong life and encourage emotional well-being as they did of the weekend binge drinking so prevalent among the young.

The Joy of Drinking

This [viewpoint] has looked at how warnings about the dangers of alcohol and exploiting negative models of drinking have a limited impact on encouraging successful drinking patterns. In place of more elaborate and intensive communication of such negative models, we may gain more by presenting a positive model of drinking. Attributes of alcohol consumption can be identified in such a positive model, such as that it:

- brings pleasure, in both the short and the long run;

- facilitates social interaction, including both intimacy and friendship;

- is associated with physical well-being and health;

- contributes to positive thinking and intellectual pleasure;

- supports, rather than interferes with, other primary pleasures in life. . . .

Perhaps the time has arrived where we can try to overcome the aversion to acknowledging the pleasure in drinking, even in intoxication. . . . In the service of this goal, we can rely on the mature examples provided by the Mass-Observation respondents quoted above, who so brilliantly describe the association of drinking with conviviality, relaxation, relationships, concentration, exercise, activity, physical contentment, and health.

> *"It's time for a renewed commitment to get hardcore drunk drivers off the roads for good."*

Drunk Driving Prevention Should Target Problem Drinkers

Jeanne Mejeur

Drivers with a high blood alcohol content (BAC) cause a significant number of roadway accidents and fatalities, argues Jeanne Mejeur in the following viewpoint. She explains that many of these people are problem drinkers and repeat offenders and insists that states need to take action to prevent them from drinking and driving. According to Mejeur, effective strategies include enacting stiff penalties for high BAC offenses, encouraging BAC testing, ignition interlocks for repeat offenders, and providing education on drug and alcohol abuse. Mejeur is an expert on drunk driving laws and writes about traffic safety issues for the National Conference of States Legislatures.

Jeanne Mejeur, "Way Too Drunk to Drive: About 48 People a Day Are Killed By Drunk Drivers. Some of Those Drivers Are Extremely Drunk," *State Legislatures*, vol. 31, December 2005, pp. 18–20. Copyright © 2005 National Conference of State Legislatures. Reproduced by permission.

As you read, consider the following questions:

1. Why do many drunk drivers refuse a BAC test, in Mejeur's opinion?

2. As explained by the author, now that the New Mexico Department of Transportation requires interlocks for all convicted drunk drivers, by what percentage has drunk driving arrests declined?

3. According to Mejeur, in 2004 approximately how many people died each week as a result of drunk driving?

All are sad stories; some are heartbreaking. Kris Mansfield survived his tour of duty in Iraq, only to be killed by a drunk driver less than four months after coming home to Colorado. The drunk driver's blood alcohol content (BAC) was an extremely high .217.

Seven-year-old Katie Flynn was the flower girl in her aunt's wedding and was riding home from the ceremony when their limousine was hit by a drunk driver going the wrong way on a Long Island parkway. Katie was killed instantly, along with the limo driver. Six members of the family were seriously injured. The drunk driver's BAC was .28.

These stories have more in common than a young life tragically cut short. The drivers in both instances were extremely drunk, about three times the legal limit. High BAC drivers are one of the most persistent and intractable facets of the drunk driving problem.

Extremely Drunk and Driving

Of the more than 42,000 traffic deaths in 2003, 40 percent were alcohol related. Twenty-two percent involved drivers with BAC levels in excess of .16. That's twice the legal limit of .08. It's also incredibly impaired.

"High BAC drivers are overrepresented in alcohol-related fatal crashes," says Anne McCartt, vice president for research at the Insurance Institute for Highway Safety. "For this reason, there's nothing misguided about deterrence programs targeting them."

At least 32 states have enacted high BAC laws, often called aggravated or extreme drunk driving. States with high BAC laws establish a two-tiered system of drunk driving offenses. The basic drunk driving limit is still set at .08 but a second, higher BAC level is established for drivers who are very drunk. States' high BAC thresholds range from .15 to .20.

Some states impose stiffer penalties for a high BAC offense, while others make it a separate offense, with separate penalties. At least 11 states considered bills to establish a high BAC threshold during the 2005 legislative session, but the only bill to pass was in Texas. The new law imposes higher fines and ignition interlocks for drivers with a BAC in excess of .15.

Are high BAC laws effective? The National Highway Traffic Safety Administration (NHTSA) says yes. In a study of Minnesota's laws. "Enhanced Sanctions for Higher BACs: Evaluation of Minnesota's High-BAC Law," published in 2004, NHTSA found that they worked. Minnesota's high BAC threshold is relatively high, at .20, but strong sanctions have made it effective. The study found that the high BAC law lowered recidivism and refusal rates among high BAC first-time offenders.

Get a BAC Test

It's hard to prosecute a drunk driver if you don't have a BAC test result. Juries want to know how drunk the driver was. For prosecutors, it's the single most important piece of evidence. It's a big problem, however, because nationwide, about a quarter of drivers refuse to be tested. In Louisiana, Massachusetts, Ohio, and Texas, the refusal rate is more than 40 percent. In New Hampshire and Rhode Island, more than 80 percent of allegedly drunk drivers refuse.

The Worst Alcohol-Related Collision

In 1988, the Safety Board investigated the worst alcohol-related highway collision in American history, the collision of a pick-up truck and a church activity bus in Carrollton, Kentucky. The crash killed 27 and injured 34 innocent people. The pick-up driver had been drinking and was traveling the wrong way on an Interstate. Ninety minutes after the crash, the pick-up driver's blood alcohol content (BAC) was 0.26 percent. This individual was a hard core drinking driver. . . .

Hard core drinking drivers are involved in almost 40 percent of all alcohol-related highway deaths. From 1983 through 2003, more than 170,000 people died in crashes involving hard core drinking drivers.

Steve Blackistone, testimony before the Committee on Public Safety, California Senate on Impaired Driving Legislation, Sacramento, California, June 21, 2005.

In many states, the punishment for refusal is light—generally a license suspension. Compare that to the penalties for a conviction, which at a minimum include a suspended license, fines, jail time and probation. It's no wonder many drunk drivers refuse the test.

So at least 15 states have made it harder to refuse. They've adopted criminal penalties for refusal that include hefty fines and jail time. In Alaska, Minnesota, and Vermont, the penalties for refusing to be tested are the same as for being convicted of drunk driving. Advocates believe that faced with harsher penalties for refusing, more drunk drivers will take a BAC test, hoping that they'll pass.

Getting drivers to take BAC tests may have broader benefits. "Reducing test refusals increases the effectiveness of the criminal system so offenders can't avoid penalties. It can also identify problem drinkers, and help them get some help," according to Dr. Thomas Zwicker, senior research associate with the Preusser Research Group in Connecticut.

Require Ignition Interlocks

Many high BAC drivers are repeat offenders. So a number of states now require them to have an ignition interlock installed on their vehicle.

The device is similar to the Breathalyzers police use. The driver blows into the ignition interlock before starting the car. If the device detects alcohol in the person's breath, the car won't start. Some devices require frequent retesting while the car is running, to ensure that the driver isn't drinking while driving.

Judges typically have the discretion to order the installation of ignition interlocks as part of sentencing for convicted drunk drivers. In states where use of ignition interlocks is mandatory, they are generally required only for repeat offenders, as a condition of probation, or for restoration of limited driving privileges.

New Mexico passed a law in 2005 making it the first state in the nation to mandate ignition interlocks for all convicted drunk drivers, including first time offenders. "It's a great use of new technology and behavior modification wrapped up into one," says Senator Kent Cravens, who co-sponsored the law with Representative Ken Martinez. Senator Cravens knows first-hand the pain caused by drunk drivers. His sister-in-law and three nieces were killed and his brother severely injured by a drunk driver in a tragic Christmas Eve accident in 1992.

The New Mexico law requires all convicted drunk drivers to apply for an "Ignition Interlock License" permitting them to drive legally on a revoked license once they have an ignition interlock installed. Drivers who don't apply because they don't have a vehicle or claim they won't drive can be sentenced to house arrest.

Approximately 6,000 interlocks have been installed in New Mexico so far. According to the New Mexico Department of Transportation, offenders who have an ignition interlock installed on their vehicle have 75 percent fewer drunk driving arrests than those without interlocks.

Treat Substance Abuse

Drivers with drinking or drug addictions are more likely to become repeat offenders or to drive when extremely impaired. Addressing underlying substance abuse problems is critical in stopping the cycle, experts say.

More than half the states require convicted drunk drivers to attend education programs on alcohol and drug abuse. And a growing number of states are requiring substance abuse education even for first time offenders.

But for some, education is not enough. Judges in almost all states have the discretion to require offenders to undergo substance abuse treatment as part of their sentences. Many states require education and treatment for limited restoration of driving privileges or as a condition of probation. Getting convicted impaired drivers into treatment for drinking or drug problems helps to curb repeated offenses.

Magnitude Demands Action

States have made great progress over the last three decades [between 1975 and 2005] in reducing drunk driving fatalities. In the past, alcohol was involved in more than half of traffic fatalities. Now it's down to about 40 percent. But there's still a long way to go in reducing drunk driving deaths.

Like those about Kris Mansfield and Katie Flynn, there are thousands of tragic drunk driving stories each year. In 2004, 16,694 deaths were caused by impaired drivers. That's about 320 people a week, roughly the equivalent of a weekly plane crash killing everyone on board. If that were happening, no one would fly and the public would clamor for action. Because drunk driving deaths generally involve only one or two victims at a time and they're spread all over the country, the death toll isn't as obvious as a weekly plane crash. But the number of deaths is the same.

And each story is personal. Glynn R. Birch, national president of MADD [Mothers Against Drunk Driving], lost his 21-month old son to a drunk driver. "MADD continues to remind the country that drunk driving should not be tolerated, by placing the faces of loved ones on the cold, hard statistics that litter our roadways," says Birch. Considering the thousands of families affected every year, it's time for a renewed commitment to get hardcore drunk drivers off the roads for good.

| *"Focusing on the heavy drinker and ig-noring the current normative drinker . . . could be a mistake."*

It Would Be a Mistake to Target Only Problem Drinkers

Robert B. Voas, Eduardo Romano, A. Scott Tippetts, and C. Debra M. Furr-Holden

In the following viewpoint, Robert B. Voas, Eduardo Romano, A. Scott Tippetts, and C. Debra M. Furr-Holden examine alcohol-related crash statistics and conclude that both abusive heavy drinkers and more moderate drinkers contribute to highway crashes. While prevention of driving by heavy drinkers is important, the authors argue that prevention programs should not ignore other drinkers who also contribute significantly to alcohol-related traffic accidents. The authors are researchers at the Pacific Institute for Research and Evaluation, an organization that focuses on the individual and social problems associated with the use of alcohol and other drugs.

Robert B. Voas, Eduardo Romano, A. Scott Tippetts, and C. Debra M. Furr-Holden, "Drinking Status and Fatal Crashes: Which Drivers Contribute Most to the Problem?" *Journal of Studies on Alcohol*, vol. 67, September 2006, pp. 722–729. Copyright © 2006 by Alcohol Research Documentation, Inc., Rutgers Center of Alcohol Studies, Piscataway, NJ 08854. Reprinted with permission.

As you read, consider the following questions:

1. What is the definition of a hardcore driver, according to the authors?

2. Why is the question of who contributes the most to fatal crashes important to policy makers, in the opinion of the authors?

3. According to the authors, after adjusting for the number of drivers in each drinking category, what group of drinkers contributes most to the alcohol-related crash problem?

A significant issue in traffic safety has been the characterization of road users who most contribute to the alcohol-related crash problem. As early as 1967, a report by the Department of Transportation (1968) identified the "problem drinker" as an important target for alcohol safety programs. [Researcher E.] Vingilis (1983), in a review of studies on the drinking status of impaired drivers, concluded that 30%–50% of the drivers in alcohol-related crashes or arrests have "drinking problems." In 1990, [researcher W. F] Wieczorek et al. reported that 51% of driving under the influence (DUI) offenders who were referred for treatment met the *Diagnostic and Statistical Manual of Mental Disorders*, 3rd edition, Revised, . . . criteria for alcohol dependence. . . .

An Ongoing Debate

A follow-back study (i.e., based on reports from family and associates) conducted by [researcher S. P.] Baker et al. (2002) gave some support to those who argue that "problem drinkers" are the main contributors to fatal crashes. In their study of 818 fatally injured drivers. 21%–61% of the fatally injured drivers with blood alcohol concentrations (BACs) of $\geq$.15% could have been classified as problem drinkers before their crash involvement, compared with 1%–7% of the fatally injured drivers with BACs of .00%. The authors noted, however,

Even Moderate or Light Drinking Can Cause Accidents

Any amount of alcohol affects your ability to drive safely. The effects can include:

- slower reactions

- increased stopping distance

- poorer judgment of speed and distance

- reduced field of vision . . .

There are no excuses

"I had a drink but it was at lunch time"

Even a small drink at lunchtime can make you more sleepy and impair your driving.

"I feel fine to drive"

Any amount of alcohol will affect your judgement.

"I've only had a couple"

Even a single drink will affect your driving performance.

Think Road Safety Web site, "When Will You Have Had Too Much?"
2007. www.thinkroadsafety.gov.uk.

that many high BAC drivers in fatal crashes were not found to be problem drinkers. These two findings are at the core of an ongoing debate about the type of drinker that contributes the most to the incidence of fatal crashes. This debate centers on the magnitude of the contribution of "hard core" drinking drivers to the alcohol-related crash problem. [researcher H. M.] Simpson and [D. R.] Mayhew (1991) define "hard core drivers" as "individuals who frequently drive after drinking, usually with high BACs ($\geq$.15%), and who have a history of arrests and convictions for impaired driving." The term has been adopted by several governmental and private organizations such as the National Transportation Safety Board, the National Highway Traffic Safety Administration (NHTSA), and the National Commission Against Drunk Driving. The use of the term varies somewhat, but it basically encompasses multiple offenders who repeatedly drive under the influence and first offenders who are arrested with high BACs (.15%).

Policy Issues

On one side of the debate, Simpson and Mayhew (1991) emphasized the contribution of hard core drivers to the crash problem by claiming that they account for more than 50% of alcohol-related crashes occurring at night. Researchers and policy makers concerned by this finding emphasize the need for programs targeting these hard core drivers. On the other side of the debate, some authors . . . have argued that although hard core drivers are overrepresented among high BAC drivers in fatal crashes, they account for only a small proportion of all fatal crashes. What type of drinker contributes the most to the fatal crash problem?

The answer to this question involves important policy issues. At stake is the optimal allocation of increasingly scarce resources. Policy makers must decide whether to allocate resources to specific deterrence programs designed to reduce recidivism among the relatively small number of high-risk DUI offenders, general deterrence programs aimed at the much large number of lower risk drivers in the general drinking public, or both. Optimizing resource allocation between these programs is not straightforward for three reasons. First, programs aimed at the drinking public (such as increased enforcement using checkpoints and public information campaigns) are substantially different from those directed at hard core drivers (such as intensified court monitoring, jail time, and extended treatment programs). Second, laws and programs related to these policies are enacted at the state level, where state traffic safety funds are generally extremely limited. Third, although the relationship of acute BAC to crash involvement is known ... there is substantially less information on the drinking characteristic of drivers and crash involvement.

Limited Data

In contrast to the wealth of information on BACs at the time of crashes, information is relatively limited on the drinking characteristics of drivers in fatal crashes. Our review of both sides of the hard core driver debate demonstrates that such information is very limited because of the inability to study fatally injured drivers directly. We used two data sets for this study: the National Epidemiologic Survey on Alcohol and Related Conditions (NESARC) National Institute on Alcohol Abuse and Alcoholism (NIAAA, 2004), a recent national household survey of alcohol consumption by U.S. residents, and the Fatality Analysis Reporting System (FARS: NHTSA, 2002). From the NESARC, we determined the prevalence of alcohol-use disorders in each state. These data were then related to the proportion of the state's fatal crashes that involve a drinking road user as recorded in the FARS. Because of the current limitation in the data on the contribution of different types of drinkers to the fatal crash problem and the comprehensiveness of the two data sets at our disposal, we believe the information provided by this study, albeit imperfect, will be highly relevant to state policy makers and useful to the research community in suggesting new lines of research. . . .

Six Categories of Drinkers

Using the data from the 2001–2002 NESARC, we developed six nonoverlapping alcohol consumption categories: dependent drinkers, abusive drinkers, dependent and abusive drinkers, heavy episodic drinkers, current normative drinkers [normal or moderate drinkers] and current nondrinkers. . . .

Based on NESARC's by-state data of self-reported drinking in the last 12 months, we determined the percentage of the population in each state that fell into each of the six non-overlapping consumption categories in. . . . To determine the relationship of these state distributions of drinker types to drivers in alcohol-related crashes, we used 3 years of data (1999–2001, inclusive) from FARS. . . . The FARS is a census of all fatal crashes on public roadways that result in a death within 30 days. It provides detailed information, including BAC's at the time of the crash, on all drivers of motor vehicles involved in fatal crashes in the United States. . . .

Both Types of Drinkers to Blame

Based on the results of this study, it is possible to estimate the number of fatalities associated with each category of drinker. . . . These estimates suggest that the programs that deal with heavy episodic drinkers and abusive drinkers are likely to be the most efficient, because drinkers in those categories have the highest potential . . . to become drinking drivers in fatal crashes. . . . Finally, our results suggest that among the apparently normal current drinkers (based on the NESARC), a substantial number of them will be involved as high BAC drivers in highway crashes. There is a need to determine whether this is underreporting of alcohol consumption by the respondent or whether otherwise apparently normative drinkers may become involved in crashes at high BACs.

In summary, this study provides pieces of evidence in support of both sides of the debate about the type of drinker who contributes the most to the alcohol-related fatal crash problem. Our results show a positive relationship between heavy abusive drinking (which, along with repeated impaired driving, typifies the hard core driver) and alcohol-related fatal crashes. When this relationship is adjusted by the number of drivers in each drinking category, however, those who contributed the most to the alcohol-related crash problem are the current normative drinkers, who are much more numerous than symptomatic drinkers. This finding suggests that focusing on the heavy drinker and ignoring the current normative drinker in the design of programs aimed to curb the alcohol-related crash problem could be a mistake.

"Kids are going to drink; it's better that they do it in a controlled, supervised environment."

Parental Supervision of Teenage Drinking Can Be Beneficial

Radley Balko

Statistics show that underage youth are very likely to consume alcohol, regardless of its legality, maintains Radley Balko in the following viewpoint. Given this fact, Balko believes that the safest approach by parents is to recognize that such drinking takes place and to throw supervised parties where they do not allow drinking youth to drive home. In his opinion, it is illogical and ineffective to punish parents for protecting their children in this way. Balko is a policy analyst for the Cato Institute and author of the study "Back Door to Prohibition: The New War on Social Drinking."

As you read, consider the following questions:

1. According to the author, what percentage of high school students admit to drinking and driving in the past month?

Radley Balko, "Zero Tolerance Makes Zero Sense," *Washington Post*, August 9, 2005, p. A17. Copyright © 2005 The Washington Post Company. Reproduced by permission of the author.

2. As explained by Balko, are supervised parties legal?

3. Why do uncompromising approaches to drinking often make the roads less safe, as argued by Balko?

Imagine for a moment that you're a parent with a teenage son. He doesn't drink, but you know his friends do. You're also not naive. You've read the government's statistics: 47 percent of high school students tell researchers they've had a drink of alcohol in the previous 30 days. Thirty percent have had at least five drinks in a row in the past month. Thirteen percent admitted to having driven in the previous month after drinking alcohol.

So, what do you do with regard to your son's social life? Many parents have decided to take a realist's approach. They're throwing parties for their kids and their friends. They serve alcohol at these parties, but they also collect car keys to make sure no one drives home until the next morning. Their logic makes sense: The kids are going to drink; it's better that they do it in a controlled, supervised environment.

A Supervised Party

That's exactly what a Rhode Island couple did in 2004. When they learned that their son planned to celebrate the prom with a booze bash at a beach 40 miles away, William and Patricia Anderson instead threw a supervised party for him and his friends at their home. They served alcohol, but William Anderson stationed himself at the party's entrance and collected keys from every teen who showed. No one who came to the party could leave until the next morning.

For this the Andersons found themselves arrested and charged with supplying alcohol to minors. The case ignited a fiery debate that eventually spilled onto the front page of the *Wall Street Journal*. The local chapter of Mothers Against Drunk Driving [MADD] oddly decided to make an example

Parents Who Understand that Drinking Will Occur

In my work as a drug researcher and educator, I have spoken confidentially with hundreds of parents who have strongly encouraged their teens to abstain, assessed the reality of this request, and then reluctantly provided their home as a safe space to gather.... These parents do not condone or promote drinking. Nor do they provide or serve alcohol at parties. But they understand that underage drinking will occur, whether or not they approve. The difficult decision they make has driving in the forefront of their minds. They confiscate car keys and keep an eye out for problems, believing their teens are safer at home where they can be supervised, than on the road.

Marsha Rosenbaum, "Procecuting Mom and Dad," AlterNet, *January 19, 2005. www.alternet.org.*

of William Anderson, a man who probably did more to keep drunk teens off the road that night than most Providence-area parents.

Unreasonable Punishments

In fact, the Andersons were lucky. A couple in Virginia was recently [2005] sentenced to 27 months in jail for throwing a supervised party for their son's 16th birthday, at which beer was made available. That was reduced on appeal from the eight-year sentenced imposed by the trial judge. The local MADD president said she was "pleasantly surprised" at the original eight-year verdict, and "applauded" the judge's efforts.

In the Washington area, several civic groups, public health organizations and government agencies have teamed up for a campaign called Party Safe 2005. You may have heard the ads on local radio stations in prom season, warning parents that law enforcement would be taking a zero-tolerance approach to underage drinking. The commercials explicitly said that even supervised parties—such as those where parents collect the keys of party goers—wouldn't be spared. Parents would risk jail time and a fine of $1,000 per underage drinker.

Troubling Approaches to Drinking

Not only do such uncompromising approaches do little to make our roads safer, they often make them worse. The data don't lie. High school kids drink, particularly during prom season. We might not be comfortable with that, but it's going to happen. It always has. The question, then, is do we want them drinking in their cars, in parking lots, in vacant lots and in rented motel rooms? Or do we want them drinking at parties with adult supervision, where they're denied access to the roads once they enter?

The Virginia case mentioned above is troubling for another reason: The cops raided that home without a search warrant. This is becoming more and more common in jurisdictions with particularly militant approaches to underage drinking. A prosecutor in Wisconsin popularized the practice in the late 1990s when he authorized deputies to enter private residences without warrants, "by force, if necessary," when there was the slightest suspicion of underage drinking. For such "innovative" approaches, [Wisconsin district attorney] Paul Bucher won plaudits from Mothers Against Drunk Driving, which awarded him a place in the "Prosecutors as Partners" honor roll on the MADD Web site.

A Waste of Law Enforcement Resources

The Post reported a while back on a party in Bethesda in which there was no underage drinking at all. Police approached the parents at a backyard graduation party and asked if they could administer breath tests to underage guests. The mother refused. So the cops cordoned off the block and administered breath tests to each kid as he or she left the party. Not a single underage guest had been drinking. The police then began writing traffic tickets for all of the cars around the house hosting the party. The mother told *The Post*, "It almost seemed like they were angry that they didn't find anything."

Surely there are more pressing concerns for the Washington area criminal justice system to address than parents who throw supervised parties for high school kids. These parents are at least involved enough in their kids' lives to know that underage drinking goes on and to take steps to prevent that reality from becoming harmful. We ought to be encouraging that kind of thing, not arresting people for it.

> *"Supervising underage drinking is en-*
> *couraging underage drinking."*

Parental Supervision of Teenage Drinking Encourages Dangerous Behavior

Dave Hepburn

In the following viewpoint, Dave Hepburn argues that parents should never allow underage youth to consume alcohol, even under supervision. Such behavior sends a dangerous mixed message to youth, in his opinion, encouraging them to drink on other occasions, without supervision, and often leading to drunk driving and serious accidents. He maintains that underage alcohol consumption is a factor in many emergency room visits because youth are not mature enough to make responsible decisions regarding drinking. Hepburn is a medical doctor and has contributed numerous articles to Arizona's Sonoran News.

As you read, consider the following questions:

1. In Hepburn's opinion, why are parent supervised parties hypocritical?

2. According to the author, what is the most common age of those killed in traffic fatalities?

Dave Hepburn, "To Your Health: Dr. Dave: Getting MADD About Underage Drinking," *Sonoran News*, vol. 12, July 12–18, 2006. www.sonorannews.com. Copyright © 2006 Sonoran News. All rights reserved. Reproduced by permission.

3. What do alcohol ads fail to show, according to Hepburn?

I am M.A.D.D. [the acronym for Mothers Against Drunk Driving] and I haven't a maternal bone in my body.

Another summer weekend, another 18-year old life destroyed due, in part, to parental negligence.

Though they seldom formally request it, our youth depend on the wisdom of their patents to guide them through the tough years.

Most 18 year olds simply don't get it. They lack good judgment earned only through years of experience.

Parents Contributing to Tragedy

But weak parents often contribute to the tragedy of alcoholic death in youth.

I am still MADD at the outcome of a local teenager's birthday party held in her home last year as parents "supervised" their underage drinking. The parents, trying hard to be their teenage daughter's friend rather than her parents, allowed one 18 year old boy to slip away from the party with other inebriated youth.

Minutes later his life was slipping away and those in the car with him were seriously injured, never to be the same.

Alcohol does not have to be consumed for kids to have a great time. Supervising underage drinking is encouraging underage drinking.

In fact, it happens to be against the law. It is tantamount to opening the garden gate to an eager burglar.

Mixed Messages

Parental stewardship demands strong and definitive decisions to offset the immaturity of those they are meant to protect.

Instead, too many kids get brutally confused messages.

"El Ultimo Trago," cartoon by Osmani Simanca. Copyright 2003 by Osmani Simanca and CagleCartoonscom. All rights reserved. Reproduced by permission.-

Are we not hypocrites when we applaud the high school's dry grad and then (wink, nod) help organize their "after-grad" drunk? "They're going to drink anyway" we bleat, so we let them think it is OK to scoff the laws of the land, of health and of safety. In fact, let's give them a helping hand. You won't get killed on your grad night because we will drive you home and you will live. Tonight.

But how many 18 and 19 year olds, having received that mixed message loud and unclear, carry on with this wink, nod and turn-the-other-way approach to their future weekend boozing.

Suddenly the parents are no longer there, but their approval of underage drinking lingers. Is it any wonder that the commonest age of those killed in traffic fatalities is 19, 40 percent of them drunk.

Alcohol-Related Carnage

I was working in a Trauma Center in Savannah, Georgia, when a pickup truck carrying a grandfather and his eight year old twin grandsons was struck by a youth who had been drinking. The grandfather and one grandson were killed. We worked frantically on the other twin, trying to bring him back to whatever life would be for him. It was obvious that at the very best he would be a quadriplegic.

After finally stabilizing him we wheeled his body to the elevator to be whisked away to emergency surgery, his frame broken in so many places that I couldn't help but think that he might have been better off following his brother.

Back in the ER [emergency room], I went into the room of my next patient, a young man lying on the table with a broken ankle and reeking of alcohol. "I was just wondering, doctor, if the guys in the pickup are hurt bad?" And now, to further fuel our car carnage, please welcome sweet-flavoured alcoholic drinks called alcopops, seductively targeting young girls. Aggressive marketing of these cute "girlie drinks" means that the average age of the girls first entering the world of alcohol with all of its adult benefits is now 13.

The American Medical Association has found that a third of all teen girls have tried alcopops and almost 20 percent of those followed up their drinking with sex.

A quarter of all teens have either driven after drinking or ridden with a drunk driver.

Deadly Consequences

A weak and foolish society continues to permit the glorification of TV alcohol as a necessary rite of passage out of high school. Beer executives would have gullible youth believe that being cool means being a cool alcoholic.

Ads that show youth having a good time only when consuming their particular brand of alcohol fail to show the kids later in an emergency room, as doctors struggle to ram a tube down their gullet in hopes of stemming the esophageal bleed.

All too often emergency rooms are permeated with the unmistakable odor of blood and alcohol mixers.

Unfortunately one of my first thoughts when another beer and blood-soaked youth is rolled into the trauma unit is "What parent allowed this mess." If that perturbs you then I hope you get MADD.

> "Since '21' became the law of our land,
> an estimated 20,000 lives have been
> saved."

Age-Twenty-One Drinking Laws Protect Youth

Wendy J. Hamilton

In the following viewpoint, Wendy J. Hamilton insists that the U.S. age-twenty-one drinking law has saved thousands of lives. According to Hamilton, almost every state has seen a decrease in teenage driving fatalities since the law went into effect. In addition, she says, many drownings, burns, assaults, and other serious injuries have been prevented. She believes that the country should devote more resources to strengthening enforcement of this lifesaving law. Hamilton was national president of Mothers Against Drunk Driving from 2002 to 2005.

As you read, consider the following questions:

1. How has the age-twenty-one law impacted the number of fifteen- to twenty-year-olds killed in alcohol-related crashes, as argued by the author?

2. According to Hamilton, what was the conclusion of a 2002 National Academy of Sciences report on underage drinking in the United States?

Wendy J. Hamilton, "Press Conference Remarks," *20th Anniversary of the 21 Minimum Drinking Age Law*, Washington, DC, July 14, 2004. Reproduced by permission.

3. What was the 2000 federal budget for underage drinking prevention compared with that for other drugs, according to the author?

Twenty years ago [in 1984], MADD [Mothers Against Drunk Driving] stood on the East Steps of this Capitol with Senator Frank Lautenberg, House Public Works and Transportation Committee Chairman Jim Howard, Congressman Michael Barnes, then-Transportation Secretary Elizabeth Dole, Illinois Secretary of State Jim Edgar and representatives of the health and safety community. Together, we called on Congress to erase the blood borders between states with differing drinking ages by enacting legislation to set the nation's minimum drinking age at 21. Congress did so by a strong bipartisan majority. I thank those of you who could be here today to mark this historic occasion.

A Proven Success

When President Ronald Reagan signed this law on July 17, 1984 at the White House Rose Garden ceremony, he said, "We know that people in the 18-to-20 age group are more likely to be in alcohol-related accidents than those in any other age group. We know that America has a clear stake in making certain that her sons and daughters, so full of vitality and promise, will not be crippled or killed. And we all know that there is one simple measure that will save thousands of young lives if we raise the drinking age to 21.

"Raising the drinking age is not a fad or an experiment. It's a proven success. Nearly every state that has raised the drinking age to 21 has produced a significant drop in the teenage driving fatalities."

President Reagan concluded by saying: "This problem is bigger than the individual States. It's a grave national problem, and it touches all our lives."

With those sage words, President Reagan signed the bill into law. All 50 states and D.C. responded by setting the minimum drinking age at 21 and wiping away the deadly blood borders from coast to coast.

Twenty Thousand Lives Saved

Twenty years later, we join again to celebrate the fact that, since "21" became the law of our land, an estimated 20,000 lives have been saved and hundreds of thousands of life-changing injuries prevented.

Twenty-years. Twenty-thousand young lives saved. Twenty-thousand families kept whole.

So many young people have been given a second chance to live and to lead productive lives. We'll never know who they are. But we DO know that the national 21 drinking age law has proven to be perhaps the single most effective anti-drunk driving law enacted since MADD was founded in 1980.

Over the past 20 years, the number of 15 to 20 year olds killed in alcohol-related traffic crashes has been cut in half. The number of 15 to 20 year old **drinking drivers** involved in fatal crashes also has been cut in half.

This does not even take into account the huge number of drownings, burns, sexual assaults, suicides and homicides that have been averted by the "21" law.

Twenty-one was a great victory for MADD and for the nation. Since then we have made great progress, but the problem has not been solved. Underage drinking is still America's number one youth drug problem killing more teens than all the other illicit drugs **combined**. And in recent years alcohol-related traffic deaths have crept up for both teens and adults.

More Action Needed

Two years ago [in 2002], Congress instructed the National Academy of Sciences [NAS] to study underage drinking in America. The NAS issued a report last year confirming that we must do more as a nation to combat youth alcohol use, including the need to strengthen "21." Based on the Academy's recommendations, MADD is calling on Congress to take action on several fronts. . . .

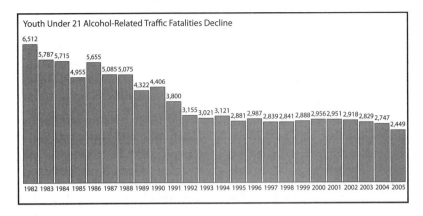

Youth Under 21 Alcohol-Related Traffic Fatalities Decline

First, Congress must educate the public by funding a major paid media campaign on underage drinking **aimed at adults**—because adults are most often the providers of alcohol to young people.

Congress must also provide communities with additional resources for increased enforcement of underage drinking laws, and stepped up compliance check programs to make sure retail establishments aren't selling alcohol to minors.

In 2000, only **$71 million** of the federal budget was allocated for underage drinking prevention. This pales in comparison with the **$1.8 billion** spent on drug abuse prevention for other drugs, the **$53 billion** in estimated annual costs to society for youth drinking, and the billions spent on alcohol advertising and promotion.

And Congress must designate a single federal agency to coordinate the response to this critical public health issue and show measurable reductions in underage drinking. . . .

A Law That Saves Lives

I wish today that Congressman Jim Howard, the wonderful chairman of the House Public Works and Transportation Committee, was here with us to celebrate the 20 years of saving 20,000 lives.

Not long before his death in 1988, Chairman Howard talked about returning home to his district in Asbury Park, New Jersey, after an especially grueling week in Washington. Exhausted, making his way home he noticed the many lights on in the windows of the homes as he drove by, and he wondered which lights just might be burning bright that night because someone's life had been saved by "21" or one of the other highway safety laws he had shepherded through the Congress.

Tonight, twenty thousand additional lights are burning bright because of the National 21 Minimum Drinking Age Law of 1984. Today we celebrate this lifesaving law, honor the policymakers who made it possible and treasure the thousands of young people who are alive today because of the wisdom of our leaders. As we turn the next corner on this long road to victory for our children's lives, may enlightened political leadership light our way through the enormous challenges ahead.

"When it comes to the effects of the drinking age, the most you can say is that the jury is still out."

There Is No Evidence that Age-Twenty-One Drinking Laws Protect Youth

David Hanson and Matt Wolcoff

There is no scientific evidence that age-twenty-one drinking laws prevent alcohol-related problems among youth, insist David Hanson and Matt Wolcoff in the following viewpoint. In their opinion, federal agencies have taken a biased position on this topic, using unsound research to back up exaggerated claims that age twenty-one laws save thousands of lives every year. Hanson is professor emeritus of sociology at the State University of New York at Potsdam, and Walcoff is an American journalist living in Prague.

As you read, consider the following questions:

1. According to the authors, why does the Department of Justice report on drinking not stand up to scrutiny?

2. Why would no serious scientist claim to know exactly how many lives have been saved by age-twenty-one laws, in the opinion of Hanson and Walcoff?

3. In the authors' opinion, how might the federal use of "junk science" on the drinking age influence public opinion on other federal policies?

In July 2001 the U.S. Department of Justice [DOJ] announced an alleged breakthrough in research on alcohol policy. According to the DOJ, a comparison of drinking rates among American and European teenagers proved once and for all that Europe's more-liberal laws and attitudes regarding drinking by adolescents lead to greater alcohol problems.

Backers of the current U.S. drinking age—21, the world's highest—have adopted the DOJ's finding as if it were handed down from Mount Sinai. They refer to it whenever someone mentions that the rest of the world seems to do OK without making such a big deal out of drinking by young adults. The "fact" of European insobriety has been cited last year [2003] in letters to *The Journal of the American Medical Association* and *The Washington Post*. The Department of Education sent the second letter to an e-mail list of journalists who cover higher education.

Problems with the Report

Yet even a quick analysis of the DOJ's report finds that it does not stand up to scrutiny. The study never went through peer review, the process in which other researchers judge a study's merits before it gets published. The DOJ used outdated survey numbers even though newer ones were available, and its European figures left out several important countries, including France and Germany.

What's more, even the numbers the department did use do not back up the claims of those who tout its research.

A Realistic Approach

Most parents could not honestly say that their experiences with underage drinking were predominantly bad. Some mistakes were made in early drinking experiences, but the first date and job interview were hardly flawless.... When adults, especially moderate drinking and successful ones, tell teens that their drinking in late high school or early college years was primarily a source of addiction, emotional trauma, or irreversible intellectual loss they evoke laughter.

One longtime substance-abuse counselor recently e-mailed me that "the surest way to fan teens' interest in drinking is to emphasize that it is for adults only.

John Buell, "Facing the Hard Facts of Teen Prohibition,"
Bangor Daily News, *July 11, 2006. http://bangordailynews.com.*

American teenagers had a higher rate of intoxication than their counterparts in half of the European countries. When compared to teenagers in Southern Europe, which has very liberal views regarding alcohol, American teens were more likely to have been drunk in the last 30 days (21 percent vs. 13 percent). And while more than half of the American teenagers who drank reported getting drunk, less than a fourth of young Southern European drinkers said they had been intoxicated.

Not a Neutral Moderator

It is hardly unknown for interest groups to tout such junk science; everyone remembers the claim that Super Bowl Sunday is the worst day of the year for domestic violence, or that abortion causes cancer. But when a government agency engages in such tactics, it gives the claim a false respectability. People tend to assume the government is an impartial arbiter, sorting through rival positions and conflicting data in an effort to arrive at the truth.

Yet the federal bureaucracy has never served as a neutral moderator when it comes to alcohol policies. Rather than conduct reasoned, impartial scientific inquiry, agencies such as the DOJ, the Department of Transportation, and the National Institute on Alcohol Abuse and Alcoholism throw all their weight squarely on one side of the debate. Indeed, they have created a drinking age industry. Research designed to promote the current drinking age gets federal funding, a stamp of approval, and widespread dissemination, regardless of its scientific merit.

A Claim that Lacks Evidence

The oft-heard line that the increase in the drinking age from 18 to 21 has saved hundreds of lives per year is another good example. The Transportation Department claims it can estimate to the single digit how many people the law has saved: 927 in 2001, or nearly half the number of alcohol-related vehicular fatalities among 16-to-20-year-olds that year. No serious social scientist would ever make such an outlandish claim. Not only is it impossible to know what would have happened had the law not changed, but real research on the drinking age has not been able to verify a cause-and-effect relationship between the law and alcohol use or abuse. Many studies show no relationship between the two variables (see, for example, "Behavioral Policies and Teen Traffic Safety," in the May 2001 *American Economic Journal*); others claim only that a few alcohol-related fatalities have shifted from the 18–21 age group to the 21–24 age group (see, for example, "College Student Drinking Behaviors Before and After Changes in State Policy," published in 1990 in the *Journal of Alcohol and Drug Education*). When it comes to the effects of the drinking age, the most you can say is that the jury is still out.

Poor Public Policy

Yet the supposedly impartial federal bureaucracy still claims the drinking age has been as successful as the polio vaccine.

An Internet search in the .gov domain finds more than 1,000 references to lives saved by the drinking age. It makes a great soundbite but poor public policy.

The bureaucracy's use of junk science is especially troubling because it calls into question the reliability of potentially life-saving information. If we cannot trust the government about the drinking age, some might argue, how can we trust it about the need to use seat belts or the danger of HIV?

When it comes to alcohol policy, federal officials should stick to dispassionate, peer-reviewed research, not slick marketing aimed at promoting one point of view. They should act more like public servants and less like pressure groups.

Periodical Bibliography

The following articles have been selected to supplement the diverse views presented in this chapter.

Dallas Morning News	"Drink, Drive, Get Caught: Sobriety Checkpoints Would Make Roads Safer," August 22, 2006.
Harvard Mental Health Letter	"Drug Treatment for Alcoholism Today," July 2005.
Lisa Fabrizio	"Encroachment of the Nanny State," *RenewAmerica*, April 27, 2006. www.renewamerica.us.
Amanda Gardner	"Technology Targets Drunk Drivers," *HealthDay*, July 2006.
Dan Gilgoff	"The Booze Ban Backlash," *U.S. News & World Report*, August 15, 2005.
USA Today	"Hardcore Drinkers Are a National Plague," November 2005.
Heather Kanable	"Turning off the Tap: Targeting Adults Who Violate MLDA Laws Stops the Flow of Alcohol to Youth and Prevents Other Problems," *Law Enforcement Technology*, September 2005.
Megan McDonald	"Locked Out? By Prohibiting Any Consumption of Beverage Alcohol, Ignition Interlocks Punish Responsible Guests and Threaten Your Business," *Cheers*, January–February 2007.
Karen McPherson	"National Drinking Age of 21 Successful, Popular," *Pittsburgh Post-Gazette*, July 16, 2005.
Michele Oreckin	"You Must Be Over 21 to Drink in This Living Room: A Crackdown on House Parties Stirs Up a Debate About Privacy," *Time*, April 18, 2005.
Robert Voas	"There's No Benefit to Lowering the Drinking Age," *Christian Science Monitor*, January 12, 2006.

For Further Discussion

Chapter 1

1. The Weinberg Group argues that moderate alcohol consumption reduces the risk of heart disease, while Rod Jackson contends that this might not be the case. Based on your reading of these viewpoints, do you believe that moderate alcohol consumption is a good preventative health measure? Support your answer with examples from the viewpoints.

2. List three pieces of evidence that David J. Hanson gives to back up his argument that moderate drinking does not impair youth development. In your opinion, which of these is the most convincing? Which is the least convincing?

3. The Centers for Disease Control and Daniel Rogov disagree on the harm in alcohol consumption by pregnant women. After reading these viewpoints, which argument do you think is strongest? Why?

Chapter 2

1. According to Susan Brink, many people do not receive treatment for their drinking problems because they cannot afford to pay for it. Can you think of other reasons why alcoholism might go untreated? What are some possible solutions to the problem of untreated alcoholism?

2. According to the U.S. Department of Health and Human Services, underage drinking is a serious problem. The department provides numerous statistics to back up its position. In your opinion, how do these statistics affect the strength of the department's argument? Explain.

3. The authors in chapter two all agree that alcohol can have a harmful impact on society, yet some argue that alcohol also benefits society. After reading these viewpoints, do you think there might be harmful social effects if alcohol consumption were prohibited in the United States? Explain.

Chapter 3

1. In the opinion of the National Institute on Alcohol Abuse and Alcoholism, alcoholics will always suffer from their disease and should try to stop drinking completely. How do you think the Baldwin Research Institute would respond to this argument? Explain, citing from the text.

2. Ting-Kai Li insists that youth drinking is a cause of alcoholism, while Dwight Health contends that this is only the case in the United States. After reading these viewpoints, do you believe youth drinking causes alcoholism? Explain.

3. The authors in chapter three make differing arguments about what causes alcohol abuse. Based on your reading of these viewpoints, why is explaining the cause of abuse important to providing effective treatment? Cite from the text to support your answer.

Chapter 4

1. According to the World Health Organization, alcohol consumption harms society in many ways. Stanton Peele argues that it also has many positive effects. After reading these viewpoints, do you believe alcohol policies should focus on the harms or the benefits of alcohol? Explain, citing from the text to support your answer.

2. Radley Balko argues that parent-supervised youth drinking should be allowed, while Dave Hepburn maintains that even supervised youth drinking is harmful. Balko is a

policy analyst, while Hepburn is a medical doctor. How do their respective positions influence your evaluation of their arguments? Explain.

3. Radley Balko, Dave Hepburn, Wendy J. Hamilton, and David Hanson and Matt Wolcoff make differing arguments about how the harms caused by underage drinking can best be reduced. What do you think U.S. policy should be toward youth drinking? Cite from the viewpoints to back up your position.

Organizations to Contact

The editors have compiled the following list of organizations concerned with the issues debated in this book. The descriptions are derived from materials provided by the organizations. All have publications or information available for interested readers. The list was compiled on the date of publication of the present volume; the information provided here may change. Be aware that many organizations take several weeks or longer to respond to inquiries, so allow as much time as possible.

Al-Anon Family Group Headquarters
1600 Corporate Landing Pkwy., Virginia Beach, VA 23454
(757) 563-1600 • fax: (757) 563-1655
Web site: www.al-anon.alateen.org

Al-Anon is a fellowship of men, women, and children whose lives have been affected by an alcoholic family member or friend. Al-Anon Family Group Headquarters provides information on its local chapters and on its affiliated organization, Alateen. Its publications include the monthly magazine *Forum*, the semiannual *Al-Anon Speaks Out*, the bimonthly *Alateen Talk*, and several books, including *Courage to Be Me: Living with Alcoholism*.

Alcoholics Anonymous (AA)
General Service Office, New York, NY 10163
(212) 870-3400 • fax: (212) 870-3003
Web site: www.aa.org

Alcoholics Anonymous (AA) is an international fellowship of people who are recovering from alcoholism. Members meet privately to share their experience and help each other overcome their alcohol abuse problems. AA publishes literature about the organization, its philosophy, the life stories of (anonymous) members, and alcoholism in general, including *A Brief Guide to Alcoholics Anonymous* and *A Message to Teenagers*.

**American Medical Association Office
of Alcohol and Other Drug Abuse**
515 North State St., Chicago, IL   60610
(312) 464-5073 • fax: (312) 464-4024
e-mail: janet.williams@ama-assn.org
Web site: www.alcoholpolicymd.com

The American Medical Association Office of Alcohol and Other Drug Abuse is dedicated to eliminating underage drinking and preventing the negative consequences of alcohol consumption, promotion, and distribution. It encourages physicians to provide valid, scientific information about the effects of alcohol on health and society and promotes science-based policies to reduce the negative consequences of alcohol consumption. It publishes numerous reports and fact sheets, including *The Relationship between Alcohol Availability and Injury and Crime*, and *Alcopops and Girls*.

**Canadian Centre on Substance Abuse/Centre
canadien de lutte contre l'alcolisme et les toxicomanies
(CCSA/CCLAT)**
75 Albert St., Ste. 300, Ottawa, ON
  K1P 5E7
  Canada
(800) 214-4788 • fax: (613) 235-8108
Web site: www.ccsa.ca

A Canadian clearinghouse on substance abuse, CCSA/CCLAT works to disseminate information on the nature, extent, and consequences of substance abuse and to support and assist organizations involved in substance abuse treatment, prevention, and educational programming. The organization publishes books, reports, policy documents, brochures, research papers, and the newsletter *Action News*.

Century Council
1310 G St., NW, Ste. 600, Washington, DC   20005
(202) 637-0077 • fax: (202) 637-0079
e-mail: moultone@centurycouncil.org
Web site: www.centurycouncil.org

The Century Council is a nonprofit organization funded by some of the leading U.S. alcohol distillers. It is dedicated to preventing drunk driving and underage drinking. The organization promotes responsible decision-making regarding alcohol consumption and discourages all forms of irresponsible consumption. Its Web site contains facts and statistics about underage drinking and drunk driving.

Distilled Spirits Council of the United States (DISCUS)
1250 I St. NW, Ste. 900, Washington, DC 20005
(202) 628-3544
Web site: www.discus.org

The Distilled Spirits Council of the United States is the national trade association representing producers and marketers of distilled spirits in the United States. It seeks to ensure the responsible advertising and marketing of distilled spirits to adult consumers. DISCUS publishes fact sheets, the periodic newsletter *News Release*, and several pamphlets, including *Drunk Driving Prevention Act*.

International Center for Alcohol Policies (ICAP)
1519 New Hampshire Ave., NW, Washington, DC 20036
(202) 986-1159 • fax: (202) 986-2080
Web site: www.icap.org

ICAP is an international alcohol policy think tank based in Washington, DC. It works to promote the understanding of the role of alcohol in society and to help reduce alcohol abuse. The organization believes that moderate alcohol consumption poses very few risks to human health and that the majority of people who consume alcohol do so responsibly. It believes that alcohol policies should be based on a balance between government regulation, industry self-regulation, and individual responsibility. ICAP publishes numerous reports, including *Responsible Drinks Marketing, Alcohol Education and Its Effectiveness*, and *Alcohol and the Workplace*.

Mothers Against Drunk Driving (MADD)
511 E. John Carpenter Frwy., Ste. 700, Irving, TX   75062
(800) 438-6233 • fax: (972) 869-2206
Web site: www.madd.org

MADD is a nonprofit organization with more than four hundred entities nationwide. Its mission is to stop drunk driving, support the victims of drunk driving, and prevent underage drinking. The organization publishes the biannual *MADDvocate for Victims Magazine* and the newsletter *MADD in Action*, as well as numerous reports, statistics, and brochures on drunk driving.

**National Council on Alcoholism
and Drug Dependence (NCADD)**
22 Cortlandt St., Ste. 801, New York, NY   10007
(212) 269-7797 • fax: (212) 269-7510
e-mail: national@ncadd.org
Web site: www.ncadd.org

The National Council on Alcoholism and Drug Dependence works to educate Americans about how alcoholism and other drug addictions are preventable and treatable. It provides education, information, and help to alcoholics and their friends and families. It publishes facts sheets and pamphlets, such as *The Disease of Alcohol, Drinking Too Much Too Fast Can Kill You*, and *Youth and Alcohol*.

**National Institute on Alcohol Abuse
and Alcoholism (NIAAA)**
5635 Fishers Lane, MSC 9304, Bethesda, MD   20892
Web site: www.niaaa.nih.gov

The National Institute on Alcohol Abuse and Alcoholism is part of the National Institutes of Health and is the lead agency in the United States for research on alcohol abuse, alcoholism, and other health effects of alcohol. NIAAA provides leadership in the national effort to reduce alcohol-related problems. It publishes the quarterly bulletin, *Alcohol Alert* and many pamphlets, brochures, and posters dealing with alcohol abuse and alcoholism. All of these publications, including NIAAA's congressional testimony, are available online.

National Organization on Fetal Alcohol Syndrome (NOFAS)
900 17th St., NW, Ste. 910, Washington, DC   20006
(202) 785-4585 • fax: (202) 466-6456
Web site: www.nofas.org

NOFAS is a nonprofit organization dedicated to eliminating birth defects caused by alcohol consumption during pregnancy and to improving the quality of life for affected individuals. It provides educational material and information on the effects of alcohol through its online clearinghouse and publishes a quarterly newsletter, *Notes from NOFAS.*

Substance Abuse and Mental Health
Services Administration (SAMHSA)
1 Choke Cherry Rd., Rockville, MD   20857
Web site: www.samhsa.gov

The Substance Abuse and Mental Health Services Administration, an agency of the U.S. Department of Health and Human Services, works with community organizations to ensure that people with, or at risk for, a mental or addictive disorder have the opportunity for a fulfilling life. SAMHSA publishes numerous reports and fact sheets about the effects of alcohol use and abuse.

World Health Organization (WHO)
Avenue Appia 20, Geneva 27   1211
  Switzerland
(+41 22) 791 21 11 • fax: (+41 22) 791 3111
e-mail: info@who.int
Web site: www.who.int

The World Health Organization, established in 1948, is the United Nations specialized agency for health. WHO's objective is the attainment by all peoples of the highest possible level of health. The organization publishes numerous reports on the prevalence of alcohol use worldwide and on the effect of alcohol on heath and communities around the world.

Bibliography

Books

Anatoly Antoshechkin — *Alcohol: Poison or Medicine?* Bloomington, IN: 1st Books Library, 2002.

Thomas Babor — *Alcohol: No Ordinary Commodity.* New York: Oxford University Press, 2003.

Andrew Barr — *Drink: A Social History of America.* New York: Carroll and Graf, 1999.

Richard J. Bonnie and Mary Ellen O'Connell, eds. — *Reducing Underage Drinking: A Collective Responsibility.* Washington, DC: National Academies, 2004.

Nick Brownlee — *This Is Alcohol.* London: Sanctuary, 2002.

Griffith Edwards — *Alcohol: The World's Favorite Drug.* New York: Thomas Dunne Books, 2002.

Kathleen Whelan Fitzgerald — *Alcoholism: The Genetic Inheritance.* Friday Harbor, WA: Whales Tales Press, 2002.

Gene Ford — *The Science of Healthy Drinking.* San Francisco: Wine Appreciation Guild, 2003.

Marc Galanter, ed. — *Alcohol Problems in Adolescents and Young Adults: Epidemiology, Prevention, and Treatment.* New York: Springer, 2006.

Janet Lynne Golden	*Message in a Bottle: The Making of Fetal Alcohol Syndrome.* Cambridge, MA: Harvard University Press, 2005.
Marcus Grant and Joyce O'Connor, eds.	*Corporate Responsibility and Alcohol: The Need and Potential for Partnership.* New York: Routledge, 2005.
William Grimes	*Straight Up or On the Rocks: The Story of the American Cocktail.* New York: North Point, 2001.
Mack P. Holt	*Alcohol: A Social and Cultural History.* New York: Berg, 2006.
Linda Costigan Lederman	*Changing the Culture of College Drinking: A Socially Situated Health Communication Campaign.* Creskill, NJ: Hampton, 2005.
Jared C. Lobdell	*This Strange Illness: Alcoholism and Bill W.* New York: Aldine de Gruyter, 2004.
Sara Markowitz, Robert Kaestner, and Michael Grossman	*An Investigation of the Effects of Alcohol Consumption and Alcohol Policies on Youth Risky Sexual Behaviors.* Cambridge, MA: National Bureau of Economic Research, 2005.
Marjana Martinic and Barbara Leigh	*Reasonable Risk: Alcohol in Perspective.* New York: Brunner-Routledge, 2004.
Richard Muller and Harald Klingemann	*From Science to Action?: 100 Alcohol Policies Revisited.* Norwell, MA: Kluwer Academic, 2004.

Thomas Nordegren	*The A-Z Encyclopedia of Alcohol and Drug Abuse.* Parkland, FL: Brown Walker, 2002.
Office of National Drug Control Policy	*The Challenge in Higher Education: Confronting and Reducing Substance Abuse on Campus.* Washington, DC: Office of National Drug Control Policy, 2004.
Nancy Olson	*With a Lot of Help from Our Friends: The Politics of Alcoholism.* New York: Writers Club, 2003.
C.K. Robertson, ed.	*Religion & Alcohol: Sobering Thoughts.* New York: Peter Lang, 2004.
Frederick Rotgers et al.	*Responsible Drinking: A Moderation Management Approach for Problem Drinkers.* Oakland, CA: New Harbinger, 2002.
Sarah W. Tracy	*Alcoholism in America: From Reconstruction to Prohibition.* Baltimore, MD: Johns Hopkins University Press, 2005.
Sarah W. Tracy and Caroline Jean Acker	*Altering American Consciousness: The History of Alcohol and Drug Use in the United States, 1800–2000.* Amherst, MA: University of Massachusetts Press, 2004.
Chris Volkman and Toren Volkman et al.	*From Binge to Blackout: A Mother and Son Struggle with Teen Drinking.* New York: New American Library, 2006.

Scott T. Walters and John S. Baer	*Talking with College Students about Alcohol: Motivational Strategies for Reducing Abuse.* New York: Guilford, 2006.
Thomas M. Wilson, ed.	*Drinking Cultures: Alcohol and Identity.* New York: Berg, 2005.
Koren Zailckas	*Smashed: Story of a Drunken Girlhood.* New York: Viking, 2005.

Index